FIRST AND LAST WORDS

First and Last Words

Memoir & Stories

by
Stuart Friebert

Pinyon Publishing
Montrose, CO

ALSO BY STUART FRIEBERT

PROSE
Der Gast, und sei er noch so schlecht: Prose Sketches
The Language of the Enemy: Stories

POETRY
Dreaming of Floods

Calming Down

Up in Bed

Stories My Father Can Tell

Uncertain Health

The Darmstadt Orchids

Funeral Pie

Near Occasions of Sin

Speak Mouth to Mouth

Kein Trinkwasser

Die Prokuristen kommen

Nicht Hinauslehnen

On the Bottom

Decanting: Selected & New Poems

Floating Heart

ANTHOLOGIES
A Field Guide to Contemporary Poetry & Poetics
    (with David Young; Second edition with David Walker and David Young)

The Longman Anthology of Contemporary American Poetry
    (First and Second editions: with David Young)

Models of the Universe: An Anthology of the Prose Poem
    (with David Young)

Translations

Günter Eich: Valuable Nail: Selected Poems
    (with David Walker and David Young)

Karl Krolow: On Account Of: Selected Poems

Miroslav Holub: Sagittal Section: Selected Poems
    (with Dana Habová)

Giovanni Raboni: The Coldest Year of Grace: Selected Poems
    (with Vinio Rossi)

Marin Sorescu: Hands Behind My Back: Selected Poems
    (with Gabriela Dragnea and Adriana Varga)

Karl Krolow: What'll We Do With This Life?: Selected Poems

Judita Vaičiūnaitė: Fire, Put Out By Fire: Selected Poems
    (with Viktoria Skrupskelis)

Sylva Fischerová: The Swing in the Middle of Chaos: Selected Poems
    (with the author)

Sylva Fischerová: Stomach of the Soul: Selected Poems
    (with the author and A. J. Hauner)

Karl Krolow: Puppets in the Wind: Selected Poems

Kuno Raeber: Be Quiet: Selected Poems

Kuno Raeber: Watch Out: Selected Poems

Kuno Raeber: Votives: Selected Poems
    (with Christiane Wyrwa)

Textbook

Max Frisch: Als der Krieg zu Ende war

Copyright © 2017 by Stuart Friebert

All rights reserved. Except as permitted under the U.S. Copyright Act of 1976, no part of this publication may be reproduced, distributed, or transmitted in any form or by any means, or stored in a database or retrieval system, without the prior written permission of the publisher, except for brief quotations in articles, books, and reviews.

Cover Art © Arastorguev | Dreamstime.com - Dream Of Well-read

Photograph of Stuart Friebert by Cynthia A. Sanders

Design by Susan Elliott

First Edition: April 2017

Pinyon Publishing
23847 V66 Trail, Montrose, CO 81403
www.pinyon-publishing.com

Library of Congress Control Number: 2017935285
ISBN: 978-1-936671-42-7

Acknowledgments

Some of these pieces have appeared in the following journals, in some cases in slightly different form, with different characters' names. Great thanks to their editors:

"Prologue": *Trans-Lit2*
"Rogue Wave": *Crack in the Spine*
"In a Dark Wood": *Bangalore Review*
"Changing the Subject": *The Font*
"Burying Beetles": *Pinyon Review*
"Last Words": *DoveTales*
"Babies in Boats": *Great River Review*
"Chekhov Inside Out": *Saranac Review*
"Tornado Alley": *River Oak Review*
"Some Lunkers": *Northern Ohio Live*
"Czechoslovakia": *Quarterly West*
"July 14-15/1998": *Hanging Loose*

Special thanks to Barbara Wuest, who got me started thinking about my "Life in German" in new ways.

The story, "Babies in Boats," is dedicated to Nancy Willard, who gifted me with the "Babies in Boats" postcard.

Aside from some names and rearranging of events for narrative purposes, the memoir pieces are as faithful to facts as yellowing journal pages and my dimming memory permit, but let me quote Czesław Miłosz once more: "And I don't know / what in all that was real."

Susan Elliott's editing suggestions and help all along: to die for! And great thanks to her and Gary Entsminger for their many contributions to the vibrancy of small press publishing.

In Memory of Gert Niers

Contents

MEMOIR

Prologue 1

How to Use 13

Rogue Wave 21

In a Dark Wood 33

Our Time is Almost History 43

Changing the Subject 61

It Takes All Kinds 69

Assumptions 77

Burying Beetles 91

Last Words 105

STORIES

Beautiful, Innocent Music 117

The Class of 1922 121

Babies in Boats 127

The Rehearsal 145

Chekhov Inside Out 163

MEMOIR STORIES

Tornado Alley 189

Some Lunkers 203

Czechoslovakia 213

July 14-15 / 1998 231

Memoir

Prologue

"We live off the intentions of our intentions," said Judith Herzberg, the inimitable Dutch writer. My initial intention in learning German was far removed from any moral considerations, let alone a reaction to what the Nazi years had done to the language itself—not to mention their other murderous acts, which a friend says motivated her to learn German. She was an early advocate of taking stock of the habits of language implanted by the Nazis, which have remained intact long after other nefarious symbols have withered.

That those years corrupted German and the people using it is deeply documented in Victor Klemperer's *The Language of the Third Reich*. He remonstrates at one point with a colleague who doesn't realize how Nazi-German has begun to infect her own classical language; and he warns that she's beginning "to learn the language of our mortal enemies and thus betraying your very Germanness. ... If YOU don't realize it, with your education, who on earth is going to avoid it?" She promises to be more vigilant, but in the very next phrase says, "I just got used to it since the *Umbruch.*" *Umbruch*, Klemperer grimly notes, a beautiful poetic word before the Nazis perverted it, had to do with turning the earth over to plant anew, but was diabolically redeployed to mean a glorification of being rooted in the soil of the Fatherland. Heinous minds were busy joining ugly welds to the purest of words. We're talking about a language corrupted from bottom to top. As just one of countless instances, take the simple verb every child learns early: *holen* (get; fetch). However, if applied to you, especially after the date on which you were required to wear a yellow star, it meant you'd not only be picked up, you'd be carted away; and disappeared, as well. As we know from innumerable studies, most people simply breathe in the language of the victor and live by it, even as they try to make it their own, blithely assuming they can retain their individuality, their integrity. Dream on, Klemperer would say.

German began taking me in high school in the early forties; to satisfy the language requirement for college, especially if studying science, or so I'd been advised. My father hoped I'd follow in his footsteps, turn to a career in pharmacy; "because," he'd say, "I'm doing this for you kids," by which he meant keeping his drugstore going till one of us took over. Gramma, on the other hand, was horrified. We are Jewish, if only secularly so. On her deathbed she asked me why I'd been studying "the language of the enemy with such devotion" — her very words. She'd wanted me to become a judge, who'd prosecute every last Nazi.

In my first German class, the mysterious Kurt Zander, who'd left Germany under unknown circumstances, drew a comical little fish on the blackboard. "My name means pike," he said. Given my love of fishing, I was immediately hooked. He was the first of several teachers who changed my life, not least by teaching us sometimes silly, sometimes lovely, memorable folksongs — one of which I'd later learn was a favorite of German troops on long marches. The war already well underway, he also indulged our fearful fantasies, for instance that German subs might be lurking in Lake Michigan. My pal Freddy raised his hand one morning, swearing he'd seen a periscope on the way to school. Mr. Zander did question whether a periscope could push through the heavy ice; and I still hear him intoning, after writing *Unterseeboot/U-Boat* on the board, "At least you have enough German by now to talk to anyone coming ashore, *ja*?" I think he managed a weak grin, but none of us seemed amused, least of all the few Jewish kids.

But thanks to him, and Caroline Bartz, who taught English,

PROLOGUE

we were led down into the root cellars of language itself. I began to gnaw on every scrap. Sometimes I think I should have become the linguist that Karl Langosch, the renowned German medievalist, thought he saw in me. I'd won a fellowship during my first year at college to study mathematics and chemistry at a German institution—likely the first Jewish student to do so after the war. I was profoundly blessed to study with Langosch, and knocked myself out in his course intended to "humanize" science majors. Among other things, he encouraged us to try our hand at writing poems off the material under study. To the point of addiction, I seized the challenge. In high school language classes our grammar was mercilessly monitored; careful not to make mistakes, we learned cases, endings, exceptions—and as a sad consequence to mistrust our own instincts, our own voices. However, in Langosch's class it was a given that I'd make my full share of errors while growing my German. Hence I just plunged ahead, even forging new words, odd turns of phrase and the like, which eventually led to a kind of easy playfulness and surprising freedom. According to Langosch, and later some critics, such ease not only benefited my work in German, but also paved the way to writing more confidently in English.

When the final exam came along, Langosch offered an alternative to the usual "contrast & compare" question, and invited us to add ten additional strophes to *Das Nibelungenlied*, which we'd been studying—an unheard of question for a German professor back then to pose in any context, much less on a university exam. However, Langosch's reputation and standing allowed him to do most anything. And imagine the release: I didn't even have to justify my verses in any critical context; he felt it quite enough to invent them. What an impetus for someone who'd never written anything resembling a poem in English! Off I went, writing dozens of "love poems" in German to Rosel H., my first love, imitating the entire Romantic canon. I'd cycle through a sudden storm to her family home in the next town, memorizing chunks of Novalis, Heine, adding Rilke for good measure, to woo her with in case my pitiful verses wouldn't suffice.

Moonily in love, I was largely oblivious to most of what had happened as a result of Nazi crimes, not to mention the German I was taking in with every breath, trying to navigate its foreign waters. Bilingual speakers at ease in both languages know there's an undertow at work in the way two languages flow together, especially if actively engaged with both at the same time. It's easy to go under in the one while barely staying afloat in the other. "The glorious privilege of going insane in at least two languages," said my poet-pal Gert Niers, who has since deepened my appreciation for the back-and-forth, the devilish "glass bead game" that can last a lifetime if you give yourself up to two languages, especially trying to write sensibly in both.

I knew from laboring over letters home that my English was waning. My German was waxing, but I was still nowhere near thinking about what Jews had suffered—not to mention many other "*Untermenschen*"—at German hands. To be sure, dark stories were alluded to if never spelled out; but in truth I was preoccupied learning all I could about a language I felt wired to receive, and content paddling off in my little German skiff— which was beginning to respond to the slightest touch. That sounds lame now, but at the time, falling under German's spell in general and Rilke's in particular, I knew nothing about what the private Rilke was writing about Jews and other minorities in his letters. Thanks to Egon Schwarz's monograph we can reevaluate the Rilke phenomenon. Hard but necessary reading, especially in the case of a major figure …

Of course, my year in Germany did bring forces and facts gradually to bear on my cloistered mind, living as I did in a dorm among "the walking dead," as fellow German students referred to themselves. Many had lost body parts, so watching the men

PROLOGUE

wash in the communal bathroom brought on fits of flinching. Most saw themselves as victims, disillusioned for having bought into Hitler's promises and programs but unable at the time to confront the matter of who did what to whom. With great admiration, I recall one exception: my roommate Heini, who wore an ugly platform boot to support a shattered leg and suffered no one saying it was anyone's fault but Germany's. As more and more of my fellow students started surfacing from nightmares that year, gingerly confronting their own acts as well as their relatives', Heini helped me parse some of the darker dimensions. Still, it took many years to come to this prose-poem:

A FOOT OFF THE BOTTOM

That's simple, Heini says, snip off the end of a Nr. 9 hook so it's nice and blunt, stick the tiniest segment of a worm on, and jig your line down a foot off the bottom. We were after spiny dogfish, as voracious a shark as any, in a cove on the North Sea, under a gray and white sky. Fall was falling fast, fish smells stuck to the air. Heini unwrapped a blutwurst sandwich, handed me a homemade beer. Perfect!

There's little demand for the spiny's flesh in the States, but it's highly prized in Germany, not used as meal for farm animals, Heini said. He's a good man, forced to fight at fifteen, lost a foot in the Russia campaign, about which we don't talk much anymore. The silence piled up around us, and my mind drifted down to where submarines used to hide. An image shot up from somewhere — slipper linings for U-Boat crews woven from hair of Jewish women; one of those facts one will never digest, which just sits in your gut like bezoar, worse than seeing that single baby's shoe under glass at Yad Vashem. Heini had wept till I pulled him away to the next exhibit.

Exactly how, he'd said, could you learn enough German to pass as a native, since your grandmother said it was the language of the enemy? I didn't understand it myself; and when Heini started pushing for reasons on that do-nothing day, I suddenly ripped off my clothes, dove down as far as I could without bursting a lung. Through the mottled yellows and browns, I made out a school of spinys swimming slowly under our worms, not interested at all, those tell-tale blotchy spots on their sides, portholes through which nothing escapes.

Before moving on from that year abroad to some extra-personal issues, let me mention the instructor assigned to the small group of us heading to Germany that summer of 1949. I'd taken five years of German by then, four in high school, one in college. Our teacher, a refugee from Darmstadt where I would study, said, "My goal is you will never be taken for an American, an *Ami*; at worst for someone from another region, say a town quite distant from where you are. If they question your idiom, casually say, '*Nun, bei uns in Wilhelmsdorf ...*' And make no grammatical mistakes! Every ending, every case must be correct! Most important, German is not nearly as guttural as English. Here, I draw you a map to use when you practice." She took up the chalk and drew a profile of a face with a large cavity for the mouth. "This little hill is your tongue, and now I make X marks where the basic German sounds are produced. Take the word 'ball' in both tongues. You Americans say it way back in the throat, so Germans make fun of your soldiers trying to speak German. They talk with marbles in the mouth, people say. So be sure to keep lips and tongue forward, for the most part anyway."

A bit of a show-off, I raised my hand. "Frau Doberheim, what about all the *ach* sounds? They're pretty guttural, to my ear anyway."

PROLOGUE

"It is hard to get more guttural than *ach* to be sure," she said, "but this sound does not occur too much. This has been studied by Professor Joos, who has demonstrated conclusively that American sounds on average are produced farther back in the throat. Use a mirror to remind yourselves to speak forward, so to speak!" Then she grinned her infectious grin, "You may speak perfectly mindless German, just do so flawlessly!" Judging by the set conversations we had to perform, we were pretty good at mindless German. Later, I would study with Martin Joos, who stomped on mindlessness and was heard to say to a colleague, "Young Friebert, whose German is not at all contemptible …" I felt knighted; but then I also felt knighted, can you imagine, when another professor said, "When you Jews are good, you are very, very good." Needless to say, our relationship was touch and go. We'd learned that as a young student in Germany he'd taken part in book-burning. Swept up in the frenzy, he'd thrown his grandmother's bible into the flames. Learning that, I tried to keep my distance, but when he suffered a nervous breakdown I visited him in the hospital. As I took my leave he said, "Friebert, I'd like to give you the one book I'd never let anyone take from me, ever. *Nein*, not ever"; and he leaned over to open the drawer of the night table. Out came what looked like a bible bound in beautiful white leather. "Here," he said forcefully, "I want you to make sure nothing happens to my beloved Heine: *Gesammelte Gedichte*. Never ever. I will inscribe it to you." I fumbled for my pen. "You know," he said at last, "our only salvation for Germany is if Jews return. To the language, the literature, to the land as well. That in and of itself would be a miracle, *nicht wahr*? But please, I beg you, whatever you do, read German, teach it if you can, and above all live it."

Live it? How? "No one is exempted from history," Richard Alewyn warns. My mind was beginning to comprehend that, but my body took a long time to catch up. When I visited Israel in the eighties, I met Abba Kovner, the great Lithuanian-Israeli writer, who helped invent the computer system for tracing lost survivors. He soon had me connected to relatives in Petah Tikva, who we assumed had been killed in the camps. When they opened the door, my knees buckled. After some nervous hugs, it was quickly clear that because I didn't know Hebrew and they didn't know English, we'd have to talk in German. Raising a glass of their best schnapps, my mother's cousin offered an ironic toast, "Here's to our using the language of the enemy!" Suddenly, the schnapps backed up in my throat ...

I'd still been writing in German, and was increasingly being read and reviewed, especially due to the support of Karl Krolow, the Dean of German poets, who'd written the afterword to my first book, calling attention to the poems' "unrest, skepticism and desperation." I had no such intentions; the poems just surfaced, but his approbation put me on the map. Three other books followed, the last with Delp Verlag. Heinrich Delp was beginning to publish poets whose work had been forbidden, and had a special interest in making a home for Jewish writers, whatever their country of origin.

To deepen my understanding of German's whys and wherefores, I also began to translate—that is study word by word a number of German poets whose work spoke to me: Ilse Aichinger, Ingeborg Bachmann, Peter Bichsel, Rainer Brambach, Paul Celan most crucially, Hilde Domin, Günter Eich, Walter Helmut Fritz, Günter Grass, Helmut Heissenbüttel, Karl Krolow, Christoph Meckel, Dagmar Nick, Erica Pedretti, Nelly Sachs, and Elisabeth Schmeidel.

An "audience" with Celan has changed the way I've felt and thought about German ever since, especially how I've taught and written it. If I hadn't met him and his wife, the artist Gisèle Celan-Lestrange, in their Paris apartment in the sixties, I might have stopped writing altogether. In and out of the hospital at the time,

PROLOGUE

Celan, partly delusional, jumped to the window at one point, peering out through a slit in the drapes. Afterward, his wife said he still had visions, nightmares of the Gestapo coming after him. I soon found myself writing a poem for him and asked permission to publish it. "Proper to do," is all he said, or needed to say.

Thinking about abandoning my own writing to turn exclusively to translation, I was also questioning my mission as a teacher. Of what? German? German literature? Translation? Creative writing in German? In English?—all courses I was embarked on teaching at Oberlin at that juncture. In truth, the more I tried to keep writing in both tongues, shuttling back and forth, the more I lost my moorings. Even dreams turned disturbing. Celan's answer spurred me on somehow; he who had lived from word to word had famously said, "There's nothing in the world on account of which a poet would stop writing poems, not even if he's a Jew and German's the language of his poems."

In an incisive article, Christopher Merrill says it for the rest of us: "Celan was determined to redeem the language of the people's executioners, a language which he said had to 'pass through the 1,000 darknesses of death-bringing speech.'" Mature poets know they must journey to Celan for the deepest understanding of how language under indescribable pressure can possibly survive to be spoken, biblically couched, mouth to mouth.

Beyond Celan, intense working relationships with Krolow and Eich, lasting to the end of their lives, have been immensely sustaining. However, recent studies have rocked me with accounts of their careers during the Nazi years. I knew they remained in wartime Germany by choice, but I never risked asking them about that chapter, termed "the sclerosis of conscience" by one commentator. I continue pondering their situations, as well as my own sins of commission and omission—an ongoing struggle, which Abba Kovner helped me frame. In "To Myself," he writes, "My fear taught me to try something else when I could no longer bear the space surrounding me. I wanted to try something smaller, like a cell dividing without fission. Not looking for answers to every question, only to discover what is nagging me. Still trying: forty years or more. Why did I want to get rid of that hidden fear?" Ultimately, he arrives at "the wish to remember what hasn't yet happened, or in the dread of what is to come, to find something to transcend personal tragedy and historical event. Something perhaps at the very center of our experience as Jews AND as human beings." (Translated by Shirley Kaufman.)

The quintessential question for those of us who worry about these things is brought to a head in a Neil Donahue essay that examines the full text of the address Theodore Adorno gave in 1949 at the university in Frankfurt commemorating Goethe's 200th birthday. From now on, no one who reads this speech attentively can have an excuse to misconstrue, or take out of context, Adorno's famous remark: "It is barbaric to write poetry after Auschwitz." As Donahue demonstrates, this was not a blanket prohibition of poetry in general; rather, Adorno was actually calling for an exceptional poetry that would facilitate an act of mourning, turn pain to purpose; a poetry to confront as well as absorb the suffering so memories wouldn't remain so unbearable. "All good poetry," Adorno went on, "is at core an obscurity, a felt absence." With Donahue's help, we see that Adorno was rejecting banal, escapist poetry, the drug of choice in the immediate post-war period.

Looking back at my years of teaching German and creative writing, most of all I want to thank all those who've studied with me. They've helped me overcome serious doubts; for, as Miłosz puts it in "My Faithful Mother Tongue": "There are moments when it seems to me I have squandered my life. / For you are a tongue debased, / of the unreasonable, hating themselves / even more than they hate other nations, / a tongue of informers,

/ a tongue of the confused, / ill with their own innocence. / But without you, who am I? / Only a scholar in a distant country, / a success, without fears and humiliations. / Yes, who am I without you? / Just a philosopher, like everyone else."

Paula Fox's memoir, *The Coldest Winter*, about her year in Europe in 1946 as a stringer for various newspapers, ends with this passage: "The Second World War caused devastation all over Europe, and millions and millions of people had been slaughtered, yet my year over there had shown me something beyond my own life, freeing me from chains I hadn't known were holding me, showing me something OTHER THAN MYSELF." Yes, I said when I put her brave book down, THE OTHER! And who could be more other than the enemy, the other half of the orbit, the dark side of our moon?

How to Use

The college I attended in 1949, whose president had close ties to our military governing Germany, started supporting some schools in the American Zone that seemed ready for reform as quickly as possible. At first huge care packages of food and clothing left the college's loading dock. Later, books by the hundreds—bring a book and get in free—to dances, sporting events, even movies in the college theater. Then the dean got the idea to send a student over and accept a German student in return.

I'd been studying some German, advised to do so for a life in science. As a prank a fraternity buddy entered my name in the competition to select a student for what the college hoped would be a series of fruitful exchanges. When I got the news I was a finalist I nearly brained him.

"We are pleased to invite you to take an exam that Professor Schirmer will conduct on Saturday morning, March 19, at 9:00 AM sharp. Report to her office at that time," the letter from the Search Committee read. Partly as a lark but also to mollify my frat brothers, who were making it a point of honor, I took the exam though I didn't crack a book to prepare. To no one's surprise I didn't win, and that seemed to be that. However, in late May, the semester winding down, I got a phone call I felt sure was yet another prank.

"Are you prepared to accept the German scholarship and sail for Europe in late August? The young woman we originally selected has suddenly decided to marry and hence is not eligible to represent us at the Technische Hochschule in Darmstadt." I'd come in second, Professor Schirmer revealed. She needed an answer as soon as possible. After she hung up I sat there in a daze. The one person I'd have wanted to ask for advice, my Gramma, lay critically ill. My parents were helpless in endearing ways, and my closest friend couldn't understand why I didn't quit school and get a regular job like him.

I'd be lying if I said I gave the matter any serious thought. I didn't even try to find out what the dickens one would do in Darmstadt at a so-called technical college. I simply got out the atlas and liked the fact that where I'd spend the next year or so was just a few miles from the Rhine. At an Audubon lecture a few years back I'd fallen in love with its landscape as the projected slides took us along by steamer down the storied river. If I'd known then that the fall before the war ended Darmstadt had been attacked in a single raid and nearly leveled, with thousands and thousands of civilian dead, I don't think I'd have called Professor Schirmer, who seemed greatly relieved that the exchange was finally underway.

I saw our family doctor, who thought I'd last the year abroad and provided me with the necessary health certificate, went down to the photo booth at Walgreens, sent off for a passport, and signed on the dotted line, promising to be in Quebec on August 20 to board the Volendam. I'd sail down the St. Lawrence out into the Atlantic, land at Rotterdam, then proceed by rail to Darmstadt. There I'd be met by a Mr. Sliman, a liaison officer at the American Consulate, who'd be supervising my stay.

Gramma had dozed off and was snoring when I padded back from the cafeteria. Her tawny red hair that once turned heads was lackluster and clumped. The treatments were doing their wicked work. Sitting there, looking at her, I vowed to tell her as soon as she woke up all about the scholarship. Get it over with, no matter what. She must have sensed my presence, because even before she opened her eyes she patted a place on the bed for me—I was startled to see how little room her once heavy-set body took up now — and pulled a photo album between us.

"Now we come to my favorite picture of you," she began, "in that little Mickey Mouse sweat-shirt I brought back from visiting my best friend, Sadie Bronstein, in L.A. I knew it'd be way too big at first, but I hoped you'd still be wearing it when your own children came along." She leaned over and put her head on my shoulder.

"Gramma, I'd ..."

"Shh." She pushed off the covers and pulled herself up. "I just wanted to sit even with you, look you right in the eye, make a confession. You know what a blabbermouth your step-grampa can be, I'm sure. So I already know you're going away for such a long time I probably won't be around to hug you when you return." I must have given her a hurt look because she said, "It's all right. It'll be all right. But there is one more thing, which is why I want to show you Sadie Bronstein's picture now. We'd lost track of each other for many years, but just last week she surprised me almost to death, we both laughed, by flying in from L.A. — for a last visit, we both knew. It turns out she'd heard about my cancer coming back and all. So she wanted to make up for lost opportunities, as she put it.

"Besides, I've always admired her," Gramma whispered, turning to show me another picture: Sadie rocking me in my buggy, the windswept waves of Lake Michigan in the background. "So when Sadie was here I knew I could talk over your interesting news with her, because Sadie knows from Germany and Germans. She was there in the early thirties and got away just in time." Gramma started rasping. I shivered while she fought for breath. "Please, I'm all right, at least for the moment. Just as you've been preparing to share your news with me, I've been trying to sort out so many different feelings. I myself have never suffered at the hands of the Germans, but when you started studying their language in school, I got cramps and couldn't sleep. It was like a bezoar in my stomach." I thought better of interrupting her to ask what that meant.

"I knew it wasn't right to feel that way," she continued. "I knew I mustn't let that affect what we mean to each other. But it wouldn't go away until Sadie brought me great relief. She has a suggestion we both hope you'll act on, but of course that's up to you."

"Well, I need all the suggestions I can get," I said.

"Oh, I wish I could rock you the way I used to," she said, reaching for my hand, pulling me closer. "Who's taking care of you these days? I see you're not wearing ironed shirts. Can't have you making a poor impression on such a journey. Besides," she said, her eyes darkening, "a Jew in Germany will face some close looks. But at least there's someone, thanks to Sadie, who can look after you now and then over there. Surely there'll be some time off from your schooling?"

"I'd expect so, Gramma, but what is this all about?"

"Patience, patience, you were always so impatient." She took a sip of water and I tried to clear my head, stay calm. "Sadie, Sadie had a twin, Sybille, who stayed behind in Germany. For the whole war, and she lived through it! Around 1936, Sybille married Richard, a sweet man, who ran his own auto repair shop in a small town in Swabia. Sadie left right after the wedding for America, but she could understand why Sybille felt safe at the time, even though some terrible things were already underfoot.

"Sybille and Richard still live in Tuttlingen. Sadie says the Danube runs right through it, but it's only a tiny stream. And you can see the Black Forest all around. Richard's family, an old, German family, practically helped settle the town. There's not a drop of Jewish blood in their veins so Richard thought they'd be safe, at least for a while. No one really sensed the danger at first, it seems. In time they thought they'd follow Sadie if they had to make a run for it. So they thought. Besides, Richard had attracted the local Nazi officials' attention, because he was a wizard at getting vehicles running quickly again when they broke down. He also has several patents to his name—something to do with spark plugs or carburetors, I'm not sure. Anyway, here's their address." She passed me a little slip of paper on which was written: Sybille & Richard Kramer, Uhlandstr. 38. Tuttlingen. French Zone. Germany. "Now let me finish Sybille's story before I really overdo." I took out a pad to make some notes.

"Good," Gramma said. "That's my scholarly grandson now. As soon as you get some vacation, please contact the Kramers. They'll be sure to want you to spend some time with them. It can't be that long a train trip, Sadie noticed in the atlas. Meanwhile, she'll write them about you. Just be sure to send them your address when you get settled. Now here's what else Sadie told me and please not to interrupt. I want to finish before I poop out on you.

"For the first couple of years after the *Anschluß*—how it gags me to say that word—Sybille and Richard lived a quiet life. By and by, however, Richard was ordered to repair only military vehicles in his garage. A young officer, who'd taken a liking to him, even invited him along on wild boar hunts. Sybille could still move freely about town, go to market, and do other errands with Waldi, her little dachshund, by her side. Sometimes she'd read in the park or watch the swans on the Danube. No one much noticed her presence. She and Richard could even attend musical evenings at the local cultural center and sit wherever they wished. Sybille loves music, so Sadie would send her records from time to time. Some Martha Schlamme records among them, the great Lieder singer, which the mailman always delivered, though one day he said out of the blue, "Is this person perhaps a Jew?" Sybille could barely nod her head and quickly closed the door.

"When the German army bogged down on the Russian front,

however, everything changed. One day a neighbor almost ran over poor Waldi, and Sybille shouted at the man. He shouted right back with such force and anger that she ran into the house, locked the door, and drew the curtains. She didn't dare turn on a light till Richard came home and found her trembling on the bed. That evening the good officer called—imagine what a decent human being he must have been, what a brave act on his part! He told them Sybille might soon be picked up for questioning, possibly even arrested because of the neighbor's complaint. Something about a Jewess going crazy over nothing at all."

"Good Lord, Gramma…"

"We have no idea … But thank goodness Richard was no dummy. He didn't wait for any more trouble. He knew that some Jews were still able to escape to Switzerland at that time, but he was not such a risk-taker. Besides, he still seemed valuable to the Germans—the officer was keeping him busy and praised his work to his superiors. So Richard eventually convinced Sybille to just disappear, to go into hiding with a farm family right over the next hill where he could keep an eye on her—they'd make up a story about her setting out on her own for somewhere, not having left even a note behind. Out of some silly fear, Richard would say. Richard had been repairing the farmer's machinery for years, and fortunately it turned out the farmer was fiercely anti-Nazi, so she was eager to take Sybille in and hide her in a false part of the barn loft."

"Gramma, maybe I should just go live with these people," I blurted out. "What an education that would be!"

"I'd like to know more about them, too," Gramma said, "so make sure you visit when you can. Sadie's sad because they don't write much. Mostly, 'we're just fine, come over and see for yourself.' But they can't travel now and neither can Sadie. Age has caught up with them, too. As for you, dear boy, I know you need to go now. Just tell me how much you love me and remember to bring my favorite daylilies now and then. I'll be under a nice tree at Spring Green Cemetery, right next to your grampa. We flipped a coin and I won the shady spot!" Gramma turned out the overhead light.

I snugged the covers around her and sang *kosinka, kosinka, ko-sin-ka* — an old melody she used to sing to me — until she went under. Then I gave her some kisses, left the room, and kept going till I pushed through the heavy doors at the end of the hall.

A few days before I had to report for a short, intensive German language course — soon I'd head to Quebec to sail down the St. Lawrence on a student-ship and out across the Atlantic — my step-grampa came over and handed me $500. Gramma had had him cash in some war bonds. "She wants you should have this now. She says it's pin money but not to gamble it away playing cards, or else!"

She'd added a little note in a shaky hand: "*Mein getreuer Enkelsohn! Alles Gute und Liebe Dir!*" So that's how to use the language of the enemy.

Rogue Wave

Ellie Klarner was already at dockside in Quebec when I stepped off the shuttle from the Hotel Frontenac, where my gramma insisted on putting me up the night before departure. Only after she died did I learn she'd been housed there for a few days under the aegis of Canadian Relief for Refugees, which worked to ease the way across the Atlantic for souls fortunate enough to escape "Mother Russia" shortly before WW I broke out. She'd had to cash several war bonds to foot my bill.

Ellie and I'd managed to pass the intensive summer German language course at our college, the last requirement before our study-abroad fellowship could take effect, and we could join a growing contingent of the first exchange students after the war to enroll in various institutions in the land of our recent mortal enemy.

The first thing we did was just stare at the biggest ship we'd ever seen. "Got to get a picture of her," Ellie said, "which just might stop Hank from going on and on about his sweet little bass boat." When I made a pass at her the last day of classes, she was quick to let me know in no uncertain words of her engagement to Hank Svenson, a fishing and hunting guide in northern Minnesota.

Someone from Customs came along with chalk in hand, marked a large X on our trunks and pointed to a gangplank being lowered mid-ship where other passengers were converging. He told us not to expect any assistance because the Volendam was just a one-class student ship now, having been converted at war's end. We got the idea, tipped our trunks and dragged them by the handle along the pier, sparks shooting up from their metal edges. The steep angle up the gangplank cramped Ellie's legs so we rested a moment, taking a last look down the long deck front to back, while others pushed past. Finally, spitting in our hands, we muscled our trunks along a series of stuffy hallways, down two flights of stairs, and around a tight corner into a general section of cabins that seemed to match the numbers we'd been given. However, we kept turning the wrong way till a steward redirected us and several others who'd been following us trustingly.

The gangway seemed to narrow the deeper we descended. Odd odors started hitting us. We were gulping, running out of air. "God," Ellie stammered, mopping her brow with a sleeve, "I sure hope there's a window somewhere. Correction, make that porthole!"

We were getting better at maneuvering our trunks past others, and finally found ourselves in the section whose number matched her ticket's. "That's got to be my cabin or else!" Ellie plopped down in front of the door to suck up some energy. "I'll look for you at lunch. Let's try to sit at the same table, if that's how it works," she said when she caught her breath. "And thanks tons for all the help. Keep that up and Hank'll draft you to be a groomsman, assuming the big lug ever stops gunning his boat around Birch Lake and makes a down payment on the ring I want." The door to her cabin suddenly shot open, and a woman having a good cry came out. Inside, a young girl was bouncing up and down on a bunk.

"Oh, I'm just the mother, is all," the woman said to Ellie. "Can I possibly trouble you to look after Astrid now and then till her father meets her in Rotterdam?" Ellie nodded obligingly, while Astrid shot her mother an exasperated look. I started down the gangway for my own cabin, another deck below.

The ship was filling up. Its whistle pounding my ears, I felt a great shudder right up through my feet—probably the engines turning over, or whatever they did. "I think we're headed for the same cabin," a husky voice sounded behind me. I was out of breath again, sweating away, and looked around. "Here, use this to wipe off. I forgot to wave goodbye with it, I guess," said a man in a priest's collar. His hair, chopped short in the current flattop fashion, was pale white, but he sported a bristling red mustache. Straddling our trunks, we were almost nose to nose in the narrow hallway, so I noticed right away his eyes were pink. And just two front teeth: gold, with a simian gap between. He read my mind easily and said, "I'm a Dutch priest, the only one so far as I know who was a former prizefighter. And I'm a classic albino, so weak eyes are a given. 'If you can't see them, I guess you can't hit them,' my former manager finally said; and I knew the game was up. By the way, can you check my cabin number?" With that he handed me his ticket.

"Glory be," I said, "we're stuck with each other. Your number's the same as mine, and we should just about be at our door." Some people squeezing by us cleared the aisle, and there our cabin was. We helped each other in with our trunks, plopping down side by side on the lower bunk.

"Now what about you?" he said after rolling a cigarette and offering me one, too. I passed on the smoke, but was surprised by a sudden feeling, sitting so close to him: something in me wanted him to know I was Jewish. So I just came out with it, adding a few words about my fellowship and all. Let them know you're Jewish first chance you get, Gramma always preached.

"Easy, son, easy," he said. "I'm not proselytizing. Actually, truth to tell, I'm in something of a theological pickle myself. Too bad I can't use you as my confessor! Let me just get my predicament out of the way, too. I've fallen in love with a distant cousin, so it's something of a double whammy, you might say. Aside from the other issue, having children would be risky, if you know your biology. Well, I spent part of my assignment to Canada with her priest, and the rest drying her tears while holding back mine. But we should make an effort to talk about more worldly affairs now that we've cleared our own little personal decks." Patting me on the knee, he stood up, feigning a few jabs at me, trying to smile. "By the way, son, I spent my last days in silent retreat, which I recommend for most anything troubling your soul."

I liked the way he said "son," though I'd flash an angry look when anyone else tried it. But I was baffled by his confession. Why would a priest say those things to a stranger? I knew of the cliché of spilling secrets to a perfect stranger more easily, but this seemed more complicated. I decided to pack it away for now, pretend all was quite normal.

"By all means, Father," I went on, "I'm eager to have any thoughts, especially yours, now—what Europe's like these days, for instance, now that the war's over." Calling him "Father" also went down well, and I decided to hang onto any friendship he might offer.

"Well, we have ten days at sea so I'll tell you all I know," he laughed. "One more thing, I need to warn you: I get up several times a night. Hope your prostate doesn't get as big as mine! I'll make every effort to be quiet, but these are small quarters, so ..." I must have given him an odd look, so he added, "Sorry, I see you have enough on your mind to deal with. I've been going off at the mouth way too long. You should see my congregation roll their eyes if my sermons go on, as, I'm afraid, they tend to."

I waved him off, "Maybe you should bunk below, Father, considering." I threw my duffel bag up top.

"Fine, thanks. Now if you'll excuse me," he said, "I'll skip lunch and see about other necessities, been eating much too heartily, all that killer Quebec cuisine. But I was up so many nights mulling over my devilish situation I need to get in any winks I can." With that he stripped off his socks and began washing them in the tiny basin. "So, my son, see you by and by. Perhaps you know the head's down the hallway and the shower-bath right next door." I wanted to thank him in Dutch but didn't know any. I knew enough not to in German.

I settled on, "So long, Father." He shook off my offer to steal him some lunch on the way back from the dining room.

"Can you believe this menu?" Ellie patted the seat next to her and I sat down. A blurred photo of the Volendam introduced the fare: sardines or liver sausage, followed by braised ox tongue and onions, apple salad with celery, and plum pudding with rum sauce for dessert. Our waiter pointed to his name on a badge, poured strong Dutch tea, and the table started thrumming: we were underway! I started telling Ellie about my cabin-mate.

"Sounds like my kind of guy," she said. "Can't wait to meet him!"

Soon we were doing most everything together. Father Feite, as we decided to call him, offered a toast to the founding of our trio. "Here's to Ellie, our first, not to mention left-handed, violinist! And you," he turned to me, "our ... Oh, I forget what you said you play, my son."

"Well, you two, I've recently taken up apricot brandy, but I usually don't start playing it till around midnight, in the little bar on the second deck that stays open till two. But I don't deserve to head the brandy section yet."

"Good, good," Father Feite said, "every trio needs a brandy player. All those fourteenth-century church compositions called for brandy solos, I'm certain! And that leaves me. Let me think. Well, I used to fool around on a xylophone, even saved the sticks. My housekeeper was going to start a fire with them one cold morning, imagine! Good thing she confessed, or I'd have sentenced her to more than five minutes on her rosary. Anyway, we must give our first public concert in the meeting room of my church in Kerkrade, agreed?" We nodded in sync. "Well, then," he fairly hummed, "we ought to practice a little more first." With that he had me lead them to the little bar.

The ship—no dolphin—bellied along at thirteen knots, while we set aside three hours daily for more serious enterprises. Father Feite worked on an application to transfer to a small parish outside Quebec, so he and cousin Monika would have a better chance, as he put it, to make the wisest decision after more time together. Ellie dreamed up lists of composers and musicians to invite to the annual contemporary music festival she hoped the citizens of Darmstadt would eventually welcome, while I pored over the catalogue of the *Technische Hochschule*, studying course descriptions for the fall term. I'd been assured my college back home would accredit most any course, making allowances for obvious differences between the curriculums; but I wanted to keep track, toward possible graduate work later, not lose ground enrolling in subjects no one state-side could possibly recognize.

The rest of our tranquil days were devoted to junk reading from the ship's woeful library, catching whatever sun came along through mostly overcast skies on splintered, creaky deck chairs, and swatting away at the Ping-Pong table—we hit so many balls overboard the deck steward said we'd be assigned kitchen duty unless we improved.

On our last day before sighting the French coast I strolled up to the chain across the bow, as far forward as passengers were allowed to explore. The ship was slicing along, and I lost myself in the curls of waves when a sudden lurch caught me by surprise, sending me windmilling, lofting my beret overboard. I'd bought it in Quebec, hoping to add to my disguise as a European of some sort. Starting back for the afternoon tea social on the back deck, I looked up into the huge swell of a monster wave just as it crashed over the bow, pitching the ship so violently I fell to my knees and skidded behind a lifeboat.

Soon afterward I heard screams. When I finally made it back to the area where tea was normally served, I saw dozens of souls strewn all over the deck, chairs upended, books and bags scattered, nothing much standing. Ellie and Father Feite were nowhere in sight. We'd agreed to meet by the large tea cauldron, so I grew worried. A woman was waving frantically in my direction. I ran toward her and soon recognized her from the table next to ours in the dining room. She was hunched over on the deck, holding her elbow, her legs akimbo.

"I see it all happen," she cried.

"What, what, oh my God what happened?" I crouched down beside her. She'd really banged her knee, too, I could see.

"You know they carry this tea kettle up those stairs, the stewards." She pointed to the stairwell behind her. "Every day, sharp, 4:00 PM I wait for my nice cup of tea up here and look down, and so many people are following them up the steps. Oh, I say, I am so glad I am up here. There is no room down there for so many people on the steps. Then it happen," she said, putting her hands to her eyes. A terrible image began forming in my mind's eye.

"All suddenly, something push us way over. Water pour from all over everywhere. The men carry the kettle fall backwards. People all hollering now, all under boiling hot water from the tea now. So awful, so awful. Then I fall, I fall down so hard, start praying."

"But where were the priest and my friend? Did you see them at all on the steps down there?"

"Oh, I see them for sure. He such a nice man. I like a priest. They right behind the kettle, first to have tea in line, I think." Someone like a medic came over to us so I left her, sobbing, to his care. I made my way back toward the library area and cut through a lounge trying to get below deck on the other side. Ellie and Father Feite are down there, maybe they need my help I kept thinking, when I saw Astrid on a couch, shaking.

"Astrid, Astrid," I yelled, "are you all right?"

"I'm scared, I'm so scared," she cried, "are we going to drown?"

"No, no, I don't think so. Feel how the ship's going along okay now? Just stay here a little while longer; I have to try to find Ellie." She nodded and tried to smile.

All the passageways were flooded with people, most in a daze. Some were comforting others, some just holding onto railings or bracing against the wall, waiting for normal sounds and pressures to return. I squeezed past, down toward where I recalled the infirmary was. A deckhand motioned me along.

Ellie was pacing up and down outside the infirmary. We hugged and cried before exchanging a word. "Father's suffered terrible burns, I'm afraid," she finally managed to say. "He's being looked after right now. He took the full force of the scalding tea when the stewards slipped and let go of the cauldron. Somehow as he pushed me aside just my shoulder got hit—it's nothing." She bent over to show me the spot. "The miracle is the stewards managed to wedge the cauldron against the wall till we'd all been pushed to the other side of the stairway and could retrace our steps to the deck below. One of those good guys broke something, I hear. The other three must have suffered burns, too. They're all in there now getting looked at. Lordy, I suppose it could have been much worse, but …"

Someone in uniform stepped out and asked us to return to our cabins. There'd be an announcement when we could come back and look in our friend, he said. I asked if he knew anything about what had happened to the ship.

"Didn't you see the bulletin we issued and slid under everyone's door? It's posted on all boards, too."

"No, sir, we haven't seen or heard anything. Well, lots of

rumors, of course. One woman thought we'd been torpedoed, but her husband started laughing; and then she really got quite hysterical."

"Well, I can tell you it was definitely what we call a rogue wave. Such events are almost invisible until they're virtually upon you. They start out far on the horizon, and despite the mass and force they gather rolling along they seem to rise up just at the last moment, and of course threaten anything in their path with sheer hell. We're fortunate the ship took it at the best angle, or ..." He was distracted by shouting down the hallway and left us standing there.

No one seemed to be able to eat dinner that night though the menu was kept quite simple and free drinks were offered. Most of us just toyed with the silverware, occasionally sipping the beer and wine. We were still anxious, waiting for news of the injured. Meanwhile, it was apparent the ship had slowed way down. Various inspections were underway. A voice on the loudspeaker said we'd be late into Rotterdam, where we'd likely be interviewed by shore personnel for our versions of what we'd been through.

The next morning, sight of land was announced. A handful of us ventured up on deck to have a look, though nothing much could be seen in the heavy fog. Breakfast was served all morning. No one was in a hurry about anything.

A French patrol boat met us when we turned into the English Channel, and some officers came aboard. We could see a representative of the Holland America Line being escorted directly to the captain's quarters. Looking grim, he shook a few hands along the way. Later, rumors started flying—there'd be a board of inquiry to determine if there was negligence on anyone's part, for starters. All Ellie and I cared about was Father Feite's condition.

Finally, that evening after dinner we were permitted to visit him briefly. His entire upper body was swathed in bandages, with just slits for his eyes and mouth as if he were a monster in a horror comic. One arm hung suspended in a ceiling sling. The doctor cautioned us to be upbeat, and thoughts of Gramma dying in the hospital back home surged. "We don't want him any more depressed than he seems to be," the doctor confided. "He's going to be facing extensive surgery, and there will be some disfigurement, alas. Just five or ten minutes, please."

Ellie went to one side of Father Feite, I went to the other. We leaned over him and whispered we'd be reactivating our childhood prayers. His eyes seemed to smile. When I lightly held his one free hand there was pressure in return. All he could say was, several times over, in the tiniest voice, "This will make things nice and easy now for Monika. Thanks be to God for two friends like you at a moment like this."

"We have your address, Father," Ellie said, "so this is not goodbye!" On the way out an aide told us Father was going to be put off at Cherbourg and flown to the burn unit in The Hague's largest hospital. Ellie and I exchanged relieved looks.

We docked very early the next morning at Rotterdam, a day or so behind schedule. The Volendam had some time of it docking. The berth we were assigned to was barely a shell. Scrambling to snap a raft of pictures to send home, I suddenly froze, my eyes teared up, and the horror of it all backing up in mind and body, I handed the camera to Ellie, who promptly redirected my gaze to the large, busy harbor. Cranes were in motion everywhere, and countless ships were heading into port or sailing down the river out to sea. You could see a twisted church spire; quite a few houses with no roofs, their floors exposed; gasworks that had obviously been blown apart; and, in a little park abutting our berth, a playground with several children building creatures in the sand, next to a merry-go-round tipped on its side. We waved to them, but they didn't wave back. It was as if the war had ended only yesterday. A few bitter crew members had told some passengers that Rotterdam was shown no mercy by the invading Germans.

Ellie and I had taken our coffee from breakfast and were sipping it down to the dregs right next to the gangplank that would take us ashore as soon as the whistle blew. We were not up to much chatting. She was going to spend some time with family and friends in the military stationed in Aachen, who were treating her to a weekend in their villa, so we'd not be taking the same train down to Darmstadt. Meanwhile, the liaison officer who'd be supervising my stay had booked me a second-class seat when he learned of our delay. I had to hustle along to the station. Ellie said she'd come find me after she got settled in Darmstadt, since she knew I'd be enrolled by then in the *Technische Hochschule*, while she had no idea where she'd be quartered. We started to wish each other "a good trip" in German but suddenly caught ourselves.

"Don't have to use it yet," Ellie said grimly. I swallowed hard and nodded.

In a Dark Wood

There were four bunks in the Quonset's room and two seemed already claimed. Some boxes sat on them, partly opened, and some clothes hung on a rope between two poles along one wall. But no one was about, so after picking the upper of the two remaining bunks and filling an empty drawer in the bottom of one of the two wardrobes, I was suddenly overcome with fatigue and crawled up to the top bunk for some shut-eye. Supper was two hours off I saw from the orientation brochure, and I needed a deep breather. I'd arrived the day before.

Only moments after closing my eyes the sounds of "Yankee Doodle Dandy" pounded my ears! Three guys, who looked more than a few years older than I, were holding wooden recorders like flutes to the side of their mouths and marching around the room, tooting and laughing. One had something of a Civil War cap on his head, one wore a sailor's cap jauntily, and the third's head was wrapped to look wounded. I shot up, shook awake, and saluted. They came to a smart stop at the bed's edge.

"Hello, hello, hello! Name's Sebastian Bauer. And you are?"

I slurred my name so he cocked an ear, and I belted it out.

"Good," the second guy shouted back. "Just making sure. This is a time of spies and imposters. I'm Martin von Ganderstein, but our fourteenth-century castle's no longer available, so we'll have to find other vacation destinations when we take you cycling with us on our holiday break. You can ride a two-wheeler, I presume?" His accent rode a bit of a mocking curve, and I thought he could be kidded back.

"Von Ganderstein? The very same name as Germany's mass

murderer of the last half of the seventeenth century? No wonder your castle's been converted into a home for indigent women."

They looked at one another. "Ho, he speaks German, comrades!" the guy under the Civil War cap said. I pointed to the third guy, who took a step backward.

"Okay, okay, we give up. Welcome to our side of the big pond. We've been duly warned we'd have to put up with an *Ami* for a roommate," he said. Before I could get another syllable out, he went on: "Call me Heinz, not Ishmael. I had a last name, but see this scar, courtesy of a Russian sniper? Hard to remember it sometimes." I gulped and Heinz continued. "Actually, Sebastian here's better off. Seb, lift up that ugly foot, show the *Ami* whereof I speak!" I leaned over just as Sebastian raised his leg, stuck to the bottom of which was a monster boot with a huge, raised heel that, I could plainly see, extended his leg down to the floor so he could stand level. I had an urge to ask about it, but Sebastian bailed me out.

"Walking wounded—we have the same expression. Can't, alas, dance the way I used to, but at least I didn't have a girlfriend to lose to sympathy when I crawled back from the Italian campaign. But nice to note you seem fairly intact, at least on the outside: guess you never had a chance to suffer the life of a foot-soldier, so now you'll never know how you'd have stood up to the test. Or even if we were the best damn soldiers the world had ever known till your guys woke up. At any rate, before I start ranting and raving again while awake, you and Martin can do our heavy lifting when we order you to, right, Heinz? He gave me a hand so I could jump down and join their formation. Four abreast, we headed to the *Mensa*.

"To chow down," I chirped. "In case you want to pass for an *Ami*, that is," I couldn't resist adding. They rolled their eyes as if on cue.

Along the way to the *Mensa* I learned that Martin had also

seen some scary combat. His U-boat had barely survived a depth-charge attack off Ireland, after which he got the willies and had something of a breakdown. He spent the war's last years working as a nurse in various field hospitals. He'd been lucky, he said, not to have faced a firing squad, which would have been the norm earlier in the war. He showed me a picture of his unit. I couldn't pick him out because he'd lost a tremendous amount of weight.

We were taking our time getting to the *Mensa*, because, as Heinz said, the later in line, the more likely you could avoid the standard menu. And substitutions tended to be leftovers from the Americans at the nearby base. "They even bring over big, fat cookies and vats of hot chocolate when the weather turns colder. They drive over with vats and ladle it out like you wouldn't believe—from the backs of their trucks. Enough calories to see you through a bear's hibernation." Heinz ran his tongue over his thick lips.

Sebastian dropped to a knee to tie his good foot's shoe. I made a motion to help but he snapped at me with some phrase only the others understood. When I apologized he spun around and locked me in a vise. "My arms can still get me a job as a circus strongman," he said in my ear, tenderly. "So never turn your back on me, sonny." I suddenly realized he was at least twice my age and more than twice as strong.

The *Mensa* was in its own shed-like structure, which Seb told me army engineers had built in a hurry to speed the "TH's" recovery. Everybody called the *Technische Hochschule* in Darmstadt the "*TH*."

"All that practice building pontoon bridges to breach the Rhine did it," he added. We quickened our pace past the last of the Quonsets on a side street lined with lindens, some of which bore ugly burn marks.

"British lightning," Martin said sharply when he saw me

staring at the trunks.

"Speaking of the night that will live in infamy, to quote a former enemy," Heinz said, "I hear one of our professors lost his entire family in the raid. Their house was, as we used to say, strategically located. Right down from Merck headquarters, which, you better believe, is still standing."

"*Mais oui*," Martin cracked his voice, "isn't that how the New Order is supposed to work? Besides," his tone grew suddenly bitter, "I think Professor Breiter was in the midst of a divorce and spending the nights with the cause in Frankfurt, which I note is conveniently out of Darmstadt's range. At least that's what's come to my one good ear."

"Did you guys notice in the catalogue that Breiter's only course is required now? He's supposed to humanize us science freaks," Sebastian added, pushing back a raft of his raven-black hair.

When we finally reached the line that was forming to enter the dining hall, I needed some blanks filled in. "Think I missed that, about Professor Breiter and the requirement. What's going on?"

"I'll tell you when we load our plates with good old herring and quark, unless your countrymen show up with better fare. But my granny would approve; she could live on herring and quark," Heinz said. "And of course our nice new *Ami* here can tell us if the cabbage soup's up to the standard of his granny's." He put his arm tightly around my shoulder, "But as your new roommate and," he hesitated, "a potential friend for life, I should mention that the infirmary's not up and running yet so you might take a pass on the soup."

We cleared the checker, who waved us on without asking to see any IDs. A much older woman, stooped, almost toothless, handed us a ringed napkin, a fork, knife, and a huge spoon. "You darlings see that big washbasin over there? Make nice and clean when you finish, and I'll stick you in my nightly prayers. And not to forget, you are responsible for the silverware and your cup, so off they go in your company. Forget them and you better have clean fingers. The plate's on us, unless you walk off with it, too. Let's assume we catch you, so your monthly allowance from your papa will be adjusted accordingly."

Sebastian caught my surprised look. "Just think, mate, last year the beautiful cutlery was chained to the tables. I kid you not. That's how much this institution, to call it just one of many things, trusts us souls who almost gave up our rotten lives for the, what, Third Reich, was it now? Can't somehow count that high. And someone who had to go round and wipe them off is now out of work. Managed to shoot up the misery index, I do declare. By the by, eat as fast as you can, because otherwise the tub to wash your plate and silverware in will be nice and slimy. Some deranged souls tried petitioning for at least one change of the wash water in our shift. Hah, what a joke. They even sent a delegation to the director's door. His wife invited them in for tea and that was that. Talk about maneuvering skills worthy of our military machinery."

"Hey," I tried, "I just met the director and his wife at a little welcoming ceremony when I arrived, and she seemed really nice and all."

"From the top of the bun on the top of her very large head, down to those silly nursery shoes, she is so very nice," Martin cooed, "but she's in a cocoon and their kids are growing up in fairyland." Sebastian couldn't resist wondering how two such different bodies could fit together to make children. I was taken aback and vowed not to interject any more little observations. We sat down to the herring and quark, which to everyone's amusement I polished off with gusto.

"Long as I don't have to make it I happily eat whatever's before me." As soon as I said that I regretted it. My new brothers shook their heads all the way to wash-up. "So, what's the movie tonight?" I tried. Wrong move again. I thought I'd better eat any more words that made it to my lips.

"Ah, Mr. Hollywood, maybe with your connections you can order up a preview of the latest film. That'd be really so very kind. Isn't there a famous producer who shares your family name?" Heinz threw my way. I tried not to think he meant any sort of anti-Semitic slur and just put up my hands to surrender. "Stick some nice white gloves on those fingers and we've got ourselves a proper Swiss policeman to make sure there are no accidents at our busy intersections," Heinz lisped. Have got to watch myself more closely at every turn, I said way under my breath.

When they asked me, albeit hesitantly, to join them for a smoke — I figured they were trying to smooth things over — I said I'd better get back to the room, what with the semester about to start. They seemed relieved, and Martin said they'd be quiet as a sub hugging the seabed to avoid depth-charges if I was sleeping when they returned. And definitely not to wait up for them, Sebastian chimed in. On the way back I realized I never did find out about Professor Breiter's course but thought I'd better research that on my own, given the sparks of our exchanges. For my part I felt I had some repair work to do, even as I felt toyed with.

When I came up the walkway to our Quonset, it was crowded with other students who must have just arrived. Some were milling around, greeting old friends it seemed. Others hugged loved ones goodbye and headed in with their satchels and suitcases. I could see similar activity at the other Quonsets down the row from ours. I was grateful no one paid any attention to me and hoped no one could smell my origins, or otherwise tell from how I was dressed, or even walked, that I was their guinea pig for a year. I did recall the director mentioning there might be a few other foreign students from Africa coming in the spring, but I was likely the only one enrolled for the first term. For now, I wanted to disappear in the crowd, at least till I felt more at home and revved up my German enough to keep me aloft.

The door to our quarters was propped open and several guys were pushing their belongings down the cement floor, chatting as they went. I was startled to hear Professor Breiter's name in the air. I seized the moment, made a motion to help someone, and was handed a box of books to carry. Quickly mumbling my name as we ambled along, I hoped to pass for German for now. One guy, muttering something about his sore back, did ask me to repeat my name. But no one showed any sign of surprise or even curiosity. Perhaps I was starting to pass as a native, though I'd be sure to slip up at some point, I couldn't help feeling—what the hell, just slide a piece of paper under every door with the facts about me. That'd be that, then.

When we reached a room near mine the little band I was among stopped, and Klaus Heinrich, who now offered his name, handed me an apple. "Totally worm-free! From my grandfather's orchard in the Odenwald. Down the road a piece. He always insists on picking two whenever I leave. One for me, and one for someone, he says, who's nice to me, by which he usually means my girlfriend, Eva," Klaus laughed. "Since she's not back yet to kiss me, you win the apple." I took a smacking big bite. I might have myself a real friend, depending. At bottom quite a pitiful reaction, I realized.

One of the other guys, Paul-Friedl something or other, said, "Klaus, what you didn't mention is how long it takes the old geezer to produce those apples." Paul-Friedl turned to me, "Old Granddad Heinrich's on crutches now, honorably wounded in World War I, he'll tell you. He creaks up from the table and makes his way tortuously into the back orchard while everyone at the table sits in silence till he returns—what, an hour or two later, is it? With two apples under his cap, looking even deader than usual." Klaus punched Paul-Friedl in the arm and pushed him down the hall.

"Listen," he turned to me, "it's quite a nice ritual. Every family should have one. Of course I plan on an extra hour or so for saying goodbye, what's the big deal?"

I didn't want to pretend any longer, not in Klaus's company anyway, so I spilled my story to him after the others moved on. He seemed genuinely surprised. "I knew you weren't from around here. I even thought you might be a refugee from the other side of the divide" he said, gesturing to the east. We joked about sending a card to my teacher when I mentioned her trick of pretending to be from a distant town, far enough away so no one could say they didn't exactly talk like that, there. "Actually," Klaus added, "I thought a couple of your expressions were pretty academic, even odd, but since your grammar was correct, down to those intricate subjunctives — a specialty of mine, by the way — I really wouldn't have guessed American. As for me, I'm hoping to major in German when I leave here with a snout full of sciences, to make my grandfather happy. But then I'm going to find a good pedagogical institute, which I believe you call teachers colleges. That's the quickest way to get approved to teach in our grammar schools. I'm naïve enough to believe that that's one decent way to make a difference. To try to undo some things we've done, individually and collectively — I mean to work on the language of the young. A huge subject, of course — maybe we can talk about it some time when I stop sounding like a mere politician with empty rhetoric to spare."

"Absolutely," I said after a few moments of digesting what he'd said, but decided not to reveal I was a student at a teacher's college. "The more I get into studying German — and thinking I should eventually add a few more languages to the mix once my German's strong enough, so I'm not just swimming on the surface—the more that interests me too. But I'm mostly here for the science now. My family's pushing me hard toward medicine or research. It's either that or get a pharmacy degree so I can inherit my father's drugstore—the one he keeps saying he's keeping going just for me. That's another story for another time, as you say."

"Talk about coincidence," Klaus lit up, "I'm really only doing science and math now to pacify my grandfather. He thinks I'm going to take over the orchard when he's gone and really make it 'scientifically profitable,' as he puts it. I don't have the liver to tell him that's pretty unlikely. At least not now, when he's not feeling in control of his body much."

"You wouldn't have a little time for a question or three, do you, before I let you move in, I mean?" Checking his watch, Klaus said he'd need to leave in a bit, so shoot. I jumped to the Breiter matter and learned he was something of an enigma, not to mention prima donna. Mid-career he'd switched from serious scientific research to investigating linguistics, which made the Nazis nervous because they'd been counting on him to come up with some shortcuts to their drawn-out refinery processes. Breiter and oil production were practically synonymous at the time. They let him wander off and frankly no one understood, or understands to this day, how he could basically step back from aiding the war effort, given his prominence.

"Then, right after the war ended, Breiter suddenly reappeared," Klaus continued, "with a long study of the *Nibelungenlied* and its ramifications for resetting Germany's moral compass. I haven't read it yet but the word is it caught Director Meyer's and the Americans' attention as well. Cynically speaking, you could say Breiter's been brought here to appease the American authorities, allay their concerns about the new *TH* curriculum. Actually, I wouldn't say this to most of my friends at all, especially not Paul-Friedl who's not a bad egg but can sound off about the innocence of the German peoples, to use his stupid phrase, but I for one am looking forward to Breiter's course. I need and want help with some tough questions.

"Doesn't everybody," I could only add.

"So, see you in his course, then. Can't graduate without it is not a bad reason to show up, huh?"

Klaus had to leave and I had enough to ponder. I jumped up on my bunk, turned the one floor lamp my way, and began looking over the courses I'd been advised to take. Six seemed like quite a load, two more than I was used to, but apparently two were abbreviated lab sessions as follow-ups to lectures. Besides Breiter's course only one other really stood out — the others seemed pretty basic math and chem stuff I felt I could manage given the course descriptions, and the universality of formulas and math lingo — Professor Klarner's course: "Hairs on Our Heads & Other Conundrums," which would get a mule's attention, I figured. The subtext mentioned that we'd be "learning to think across boundaries that normally keep humans isolated, one from another." I was hooked! Just as I switched off the light and turned over for my first night on the three-section straw mattress, I could hear my roomies coming down the hall, singing a folksong I'd been taught in elementary German. It sounded way too loud, not to mention off-key, and they were marching in step to it, or so it sounded — "*Und das heißt ... Erika!*" followed me into troubled dreams of German soldiers marching goose-step in a dark wood, but cradling their voices as if in a church choir.

Our Time is Almost History

Early in the morning of my first day of classes at the *Technische Hochschule* in Darmstadt, a stream of basically nude males of all shapes and sizes, some as old as thirty or forty, poured into the large, common washroom at the far end of the Quonset. From the looks of the bodies, everyone who could at least walk was jammed in at the trough-like basins and it was a while before I could wedge in. It was hard not to stare at the frightening array of wounds all around. A few guys were missing limbs altogether, but most had scars of some sort somewhere. I didn't see Martin and Klaus, but Sebastian turned up across from me on the other side of the faucet we'd be sharing, nodding sleepily. He lifted himself up somehow so that the stump of his leg was right under the faucet.

"I'd be grateful if you turned it on full force," he said. "I need both hands to get a good scrub going." The water was so cold it burned my hands. Sebastian doused his head and shook the water off like a dog. "Guess I'll see you this afternoon in Professor Breiter's famous course. I'd sit up front but off to the side if I were you. He whispers sometimes and tends to grill people sitting right under his nose. Anyway, that's the buzz. But get there early, it'll be a scene." I thanked him, resisting an urge to help him with his platform shoe. Just then Klaus tapped me on the shoulder.

"Time's up. Move on, private. There are officers of the vanquished German army waiting in line, can't have that. Just brush your teeth with soap on your finger on the way to class." He put a burly arm half around my neck and spun me around. The scar down his arm looked like lightning. "March!" he said gruffly. "And behave till I can keep an eye on you in Breiter's lecture."

Professor Klarner's "conundrum" course was first up. I just had time to dash by the *Mensa* and grab a roll, wash it down with a cup of nasty malt-coffee, and blow a kiss at Frau Einmann who ran the mess hall. Even the oldest students responded to her like a mother. She called after me, "Wait, I fix you a nice piece of bread with butter and sugar for later. I do not want any of my boys sent to their rooms for falling asleep in class from hunger!" I made a note to write home about her. Her husband, killed in combat, was said to be part Jewish. I wondered if I'd ever be able to ask her about some "things."

Professor Klarner stared at me till I found a seat near the back and sat down as quietly as I could. There was quite a breeze blowing in through several windows that weren't merely open—they simply didn't exist. More like holes in the wall, and some tools were scattered on the floor underneath. Only a handful of students sat draped about the large lecture hall, mostly against the back wall.

"As I was saying before our young American friend decided to join us," Professor Klarner said all too sweetly, "given that there are no more than perhaps 75,000 humans still alive in and around Darmstadt, what is the probability that at least two of them have exactly the same number of hairs on their heads? And please, no insipid jokes about baldness factoring into the problem I'm posing. This is your first assignment. Please confine your answer to one sheet of regular-size paper. It is due next Monday before class begins. You may expect a question a week of this nature, and they will account for 25 percent of your final grade."

After the other students finished taking down the assignment, everyone looked my way. I kept my eyes on the board where Klarner was starting to scribble some equations. So, I thought,

I guess the word's out that an American has landed in enemy territory.

For the rest of the session Klarner clipped along, and I had pages of notes when he ended his lecture. He stopped me at the door. "I trust I didn't embarrass you by identifying you so publicly? Director Meyers thought the other students might want to attach a living presence to the rumor that an American has come to spend a year with us, so I thought it would help you get connected with the others more quickly. As for me, I am honored to have you in my course. I don't mind telling you I have great respect for you Americans. You people know how to win a war! And please, give me every chance to answer any questions you may have, *ja*?" I assured him I'd give him every opportunity to help me pass his course. He didn't laugh or smile, just shook my hand stiffly, and walked out the door I held open.

Between Klarner and Breiter, on alternating days, there'd be chemistry and math courses, both of which didn't meet till the following week. I was ostensibly there to concentrate on studies that would help me apply for medical school eventually, and the *TH* was among the leading remaining German institutions, so I was told to count my lucky stars by any number of higher-ups. With time for a stroll out to the little pond behind the main building, still pretty much intact, I found some students snacking and feeding the ducks. Martin and Klaus were coming down the other walkway and our paths crossed.

"Hope you haven't flunked out yet," Martin said good-naturedly. I told him about the mood in Klarner's course. "Klarner's a queer duck," Martin said. "Pretty harmless but goes off on some strange tangents. He'll never attract many majors. Used to teach at a *Gymnasium* in Passau, and some say he was a *Hitlerjugend*-something-or-other. He dreams up these weird riddles and thinks they're the key to the universe, or multiverse as he'd put it."

"He's in pretty tight with someone on Meyers' staff," Klaus went on, "but I think his best work may truly be ahead of him. Some guys I respect got going on some nifty projects last term under his supervision. He trusts intuition. He also reportedly has ties to some companies that have hired a few of his pets, so …"

"Well, my detective agency will keep an eye on him," I said. They laughed and were off to some sort of engineering course. I needed a haircut and figured there'd just be enough time before Breiter's late afternoon introductory lecture. I'd seen *Friseur* on a shop around the corner, checked my wallet for money, and nodded at a student passing by who'd also been in Klarner's class, I realized. She was carrying a cup and munching, unmistakably, on a Twinkie! I'd had enough of them in my time to spot a Twinkie anywhere, so I couldn't resist stopping her.

"Ah, excuse me, I'm conducting a poll to see why people eat that thing you've got there." When she realized I was joking she pointed back the way I'd come.

"Find out for yourself. Your soldiers are distributing them in great quantities and each one comes with a free cup of cocoa, but only if you smile sweetly and are very polite. See you!"

And are as striking looking as any female I've ever seen, I thought to myself, but had to give up trying to keep up with her. She was fairly loping down a long hill by now. Obviously I wasn't in her immediate plans, alas. But I was sort of curious how *Schulspeisung* worked, which is what Mr. Sliman had called it when telling me about the local battalion's habit of distributing snacks and drinks all over campus. He was the liaison officer at the American Consulate who'd be supervising my stay. Sauntering back, I was surprised to see Mr. Sliman ladling out cocoa from the back of an army truck in person, next to a soldier passing out Twinkies to all out-stretched hands. Even some professors lined up for the free calories.

No time for a haircut left, I hurried back to the bunker-like building where Breiter would be lecturing. Though it was pretty early, half the seats were already taken. I caught sight of Klaus waving to me from one side, pointing to a seat beside him, just as Sebastian and Martin hailed me from the other side of the hall. I hesitated for a split second when a hand came at me from the second row in, holding half a big fat Twinkie, the gooey white filling oozing out. Like a clown I grabbed it, mashing it into my mouth. Then I saw her laugh and motion me to her side, to a chorus of boos from all the guys around.

"You're turning into my savior," I said. I spelled out my first name and let drop that my mother happened to love Schiller, whose play *Mary Stuart* she'd practically memorized. Too late I sensed it was a tacky way to introduce myself, but she let it go. "And let's see," I added quickly, "yours is Britta, or Ilse, or, wait, I've got it, Renate! If I'm wrong, you win a prize. I used to guess names, ages, and weights at the fair one summer back in Wisconsin, in case you were thinking of calling the nursing home to report an escaped patient." I liked the way she looked at me — the way you might at a naughty child. Then she shook my hand hard, pushed her glasses up her high forehead, and tilted her head to the side like a bird eyeing a worm before she wiped some Twinkie off the corner of my mouth with her finger.

"I want that prize. Name's Ingeborg, and if you get my age and weight wrong I get half of what you own, understood?" Buttery hair, thin nose and lips, almost no eyebrows — I was reminded of uncle Max's albino look! — set in an otherwise fleshy round face: she started fingering a stark cross around her neck, giving it a twist when I squeezed in next to her. "You seem so young, some kind of boy genius, is that it?" she said, proceeding to sketch me with a huge head on a stick body, which she then signed and dated with a flourish on the notepad on my desktop.

Yikes, I thought, this is not exactly my kind of girl and I'm not sure I can keep up, but I like the trail so far, all right. I tried to seem totally relaxed and casually drew a crude frame around my portrait, promising to tack it up on all the walls of my life. Meanwhile, I hadn't noticed that the hall was overflowing now, with some students sitting on the floor between the aisles.

"Ingeborg," I said softly, "it's almost twenty after, is Breiter going to show up at all?"

"Anybody else, we'd have left by now," she said. "We're normally just required to wait the traditional quarter-hour—*akademisches Viertel* we call it—as a courtesy. But it all depends on the professor's reputation. I do think no one's going to leave today unless there's a death announcement." She went on playing with her cross, and I went back over my Klarner lecture notes to pass the time. Finally, fifteen minutes before the hour was up, a priestly looking man with a large scarf wrapped around his neck stepped into the room, closed the door ever so quietly behind him, seemed to lock it, and took baby steps to the lectern, all the while peering at us through horn-rimmed glasses, his head turned sharply to the left as he inched by our long rows. He seemed to be counting us and wrote something down when he reached the little stage with its lectern.

"Let's see," he began in a deep voice, "in Hegel's day I'd be paid per head. Fifty-seven of you, hmm ... I think I'll retire when we finish. Make that *if* we finish with our business here." A nervous twitter circled the room. I didn't dare look at her but I felt Ingeborg crossing and re-crossing her legs, then shifting around in her seat. She began a serious doodle.

Professor Breiter slowly unwound his scarf with one hand and reached into his battered briefcase with the other. Out came a Twinkie, which he held up high! "I have already posted my letter of gratitude to President Truman. I urge you to do so as well if you come by one of these remarkable, utterly American concoctions. It is so fortifying I may be able to skip my dinner, to devote myself wholeheartedly to rereading *Das Nibelungenlied* for the—let me have a minute here—ah yes, fifty-seventh time, which means of course I have in effect read it for each of you. So you might easily conclude, if you were as foolish as Hagen, a character you will probably come to admire even as he repulses you, that there are short-cuts to honoring one's duty. Let me just note that those of you who want to impress me will want to read the only text we shall explore all term long as if your life depended on it.

"Now, as those of you know who have been looking at your expensive Swiss watches, our time is almost history. Please come prepared to discuss *just* the first twenty lines next time. An average student among you would, I estimate, have to set aside some six hours to do so satisfactorily enough, and that is not accounting for memorizing them. And do not overlook the fact that this work is only a fragment, which should affect how you think about everything.

"Ladies and gentlemen, I am going now. For unknown reasons, they lock this particular excuse for a building promptly at 6:00 PM, so I urge you to leave soon, if not in my immediate company." Back around his oddly long neck went the scarf. Everyone waited without a sound until he cleared the door.

"He's a painting by Modigliani, isn't he now," Ingeborg said, doubling the length of his neck in her caricature. "If I were eating in the *Mensa* tonight I'd let you wash my silverware. As it is, however, I have to drop in on my aunt, who's not feeling well. When she gets better I'll run you by her, see if she approves."

"That's what I call a reasonable proposition," I said. She shook my hand lightly, walked off slowly at first, but then broke into a run, waving back at me over her shoulder. She knew I wouldn't take my eyes off her till she turned the corner.

By the time Saturday rolled around I'd only seen Ingeborg

once more, and at a distance at that. I waved, but when she didn't wave back I told myself it was her weak eyes. I spent the whole morning and most of the afternoon reviewing the first week's materials and notes. The math and chemistry loads were going to be tough enough, but I felt confident about my chances of getting through without embarrassing any of my teachers at home. Klarner's strange course would demand more associative thinking, as he couched it, than we were likely used to, or even exposed to, which he said neutrally, his palms upturned. But with Ingeborg also aboard I thought I'd have something of a lifeline, depending. She intrigued me more and more, but I also felt I could get in over my head. I'd frankly had next to no experience with steady girlfriends except for Helen, the hawker in the next booth at the Wisconsin fair. Some heavy-duty petting was as far as we'd gone, to my relief and no doubt hers as well.

As for Breiter's course, I did find I could read modern and contemporary German almost as easily as English, looking up the occasional word to be sure. However, I was really having a hard time moving back and forth between medieval grammar and my daily forays into colloquial German. Breiter simply expected us to develop the essential tools on our own to unlock the text's grammar secrets, while he honed in on the fine points like a surgeon exposing a body's innards without letting the patient bleed to death. I was eager to see how he'd bring his linguistic acumen to bear on the literary and philosophical aspects, hoping I'd be up to seeing what he saw.

Klaus happened to trundle by while I was brooding away and leaned over my shoulder. "Here, let me show you how that verb works, and consequently how the whole clause is put together." An hour later he patted me on the head. "Courage," he said with a French accent, "if it takes me a while to pick my way through the knots, you're likely to need at least as much time, so relax. Your German's decent, but not that good. Not yet anyway.

Sorry, old buddy!

"Oops, I almost forgot my date with, yes, Roswitha, who's finally caved in to my charms," he chirped, "and don't you have a concert to attend?" I'd forgotten that Mr. Sliman and his wife had invited me to a concert at the famous *Orangerie* in town.

"Oh my God, Klaus, would you follow me around all week please? A personal valet would make a difference in this life. I'll pay you in Twinkies!"

The *Technische Hochschule* in Darmstadt, which Wisconsin State had adopted as a sister-college, was once one of Germany's major institutions of higher learning, and we somehow hoped to help it return to its former days of glory. After settling in to what served as a temporary dorm of sorts, I was trying to catch my bearings, not mess up straight off and embarrass Wisconsin State's selection committee, when shock waves sent me to the infirmary for a few days: my roommates had begun recounting in gruesome detail the fateful bombing raids on Darmstadt by RAF bombers. They were said to be the worst, after Dresden and Hamburg, and left ruins it would take years to clear. The rumor ran that a secret weapon was even at that late juncture being developed in Merck's labyrinth of labs. "Just an excuse to pay us back for atrocities our troops inflicted," some said. When I recovered, my roomies, Martin von Ganderstein, Klaus Franck, Sebastian Plok, and Heinz Gruber were thoughtful about not bringing up that "night of sheer hell" again.

The next few weeks everyone seemed dug in on courses and related obligations. My roomies, heading toward matriculation exams in the spring, were barely around. When they were, they seemed less and less curious about my comings and goings, which was fine with me. Klaus and Sebastian could have been twins now, with Martin less of a third wheel on their machine. Martin made some overtures to pair off but then he'd slip, mumbling something odd about Jews in general and my habits in particular, so I backed off. I decided not to risk working through his behavior for now, but when I asked Ingeborg to parse the situation, she said Martin was "deeper" than I gave him credit for. She advised me to look for some opportunity to reach more of an "understanding" with him.

"All of our *von* folks in my experience have some genuine decency in them, if sub-surface," she continued, "so that when tapped they usually come through in noble ways. But I'm starting to sound like my sociology professor now." I'd barely remembered his surname: von Ganderstein…

Then Ingeborg began disappearing more and more, saying something about her sick aunt needing every minute of her spare time, until I kidded her in Klarner's class about having seen her from afar in Klaus's "excellent company."

"Even if you had any real reason to be jealous," she huffed, "it doesn't become you to spy on me. Really, you're showing your age again." I didn't dare tack on that I'd also seen her and Klaus getting on a train for Mainz when I happened to be at the station to buy an American newspaper—which one could get only at the kiosk there—and that was after she'd told me she was in a rush to visit her aunt again, who, I knew full well, lived in the opposite direction.

My jealousy did get the best of me after Klaus and Ingeborg presented a solution together to the initial riddle Klarner had posed in our first session. Klarner heaped praise on them for cooperating, which he noted Germans had better get better at, or else. I'd worked hard trying to come up with an answer to the wicked weekly riddle and wished I'd had the brains to ask another brain for help. When Ingeborg concluded their presentation, Klarner led the applause. I tried to join in but my hands just managed to flop together.

"So, ladies and gentlemen," Klarner said, "I hope you will all strive in future for such elegant solutions. What could be simpler than your colleagues' approach in this instance? — and recall that the best science is often the simplest way through the maze of possibilities. The key, of course, as it often is in most of life's exigencies, is being able to formulate the decisive question at the outset of your investigations. So, to turn to a medical student friend, as they did, for a sense of how many hairs the average human head can support, and then realize that that number is less than the number of inhabitants in our sorry city, led to the inevitable conclusion: of course there must be at least two people with exactly the same number of hairs on their heads!" All I could manage at that moment was a silly doodle of Ingeborg and Klaus examining each other's heads. I woke up enough to catch sight of Ingeborg leaving the room with Professor Klarner, and Klaus, to my surprise, coming my way.

"So, pal, Roswitha says her girlfriend would really like to meet an American Jew because she claims she herself is part Jewish somewhere in her lineage. But Ingeborg says she's not finished growing you up, so don't be in too dumb a hurry to make really dumb assumptions, dummy. Need a beer now? That's where I'm headed." I got up dazed, and followed him out to the street.

"First things first," Klaus said when we clinked glasses, "Ingeborg's aunt is not the only ill person she's worrying about. Uwe, her poor brother, has been having terrible nightmares since returning home from the front when the war ended. When she heard Uwe and I had been in the same regiment at one point — though I hardly knew him, we were too busy shooting and being shot at — she asked if I'd go see him, talk to him, try to convince him to get some sort of psychological help. That's why she's been going to Mainz, you dodo." I couldn't wait for him to finish and hung my head.

"Uwe thinks he can work things out eventually. He's very

stubborn, very Catholic too. He works as a caretaker at the cathedral in Mainz. I've urged him to talk to the bishop, at least, whose quarters he even cleans, for God sake. But he won't, at least not yet—says he's not ready to take that step. It's eating Ingeborg up as you might imagine, once you stop thinking about yourself and …"

"Okay, all right already, Klaus, I definitely had that coming. Should I write her a note, or what?"

"Hey, I work with only one troubled soul at a time, pal. But I can say she's worth all your efforts to make amends, in my humble opinion, so I'd find a way if I were you. Think of it as a Klarnerian assignment! Got to go now or Breiter will be all over me for not keeping up. He's got a nose for sluggards. Incidentally, I did notice that you've been responding to his jabs pretty well, though I leap to note he's really taking it easy on you, must be your privileged status." He ducked under my jab. "Who knows," he let me have it again, "you may even be in like Flynn already!" Klaus stuck out his chest. "How's my American slang! Resourceful is as resourceful does; something like that, anyway. But now onto my own confession: Roswitha's sister dates one of your officers, from Tuscaloosa—feels like brushing my teeth to say it. He thinks I'll soon pass for an *Ami* from Alabama! Anyway, we get to sit in the back seat on, how do you say, 'double-dates'?"

"Klaus, you're on your frigging way. Try that modifier out on Mr. Officer, but duck!"

I grabbed his arm till I remembered it was filled with shrapnel. He winced, said *fatal* with a thick Southern accent, and slumped to the ground. I thought he had a heart attack and so did the kiosk guy who ran to his side.

Klaus opened an eye, slyly. "Great lingo, Alabama-German; use a word like *fatal* and it can literally mean only one thing. Here, help me up, you yo-yos." We didn't bother to explain yo-yo to the vendor, who put a finger to his temple and drew circles. Klaus took off in a trot but I had another beer to think things over. The vendor said it was on him, poured it foaming into a paper cup, closed the grille to his kiosk and, shaking his head, took off as well.

Ingeborg needed another respite from me, I decided, so I went to the lab to run another test on the week's assignment. We had been given substances to identify. "It's far more important to develop a logical approach than actually pin your substance down," the instructions read, but I was eager to find out what the chalky white substance in my tube really was, hang the approach. When I reached my station I was surprised to see Professor Breiter talking to our instructor at her desk. A comely woman with very long hair, she'd keep pulling it over one shoulder, toying with it. When he leaned closer to say something in her ear, he caught sight of me, patted her hand, and motioned me to follow him out to the corridor. She reddened visibly and disappeared into the stockroom.

"How fortunate to meet you here," he said evenly. "The director's secretary said I might find you battling the elements in the laboratory. Elsbeth can be quite funny, can't she now?

"Well, I have been impressed with your dedication in my course, young man. For a foreigner, an American at that, you have a mysterious knack for the language of my old relatives, the Nibelungs." He seemed to enjoy counting them among his ancestors, because he said again, "Yes, my old relatives. You know, I spend most of my time these days in their frightening company." Now he and I both laughed quite heartily. "But perhaps," he went on, "I catch you at a bad time, *ja*? I realize you have other interests, not to say obligations, though students say I sometimes want them all to become linguistic philosophers, or something like that. And of course demand far too much work. A good excuse for when they fail other courses, don't you agree?"

"No, no, Professor, I was just going to put in a little extra time. Just to tread water, one might say. I'm really happy to hear you feel I'm coming along all right, on the trail of the Nibelungs." As soon as I said that I regretted my dim-witted attempt to joke about his turf.

"Quite right," he said, "it *is* a sort of Western come to think! Perhaps Hollywood will take an interest in the subject some day and sign us both on as advisers. That would be hard to refuse. But you agree with me, don't you: we must not let them give it a happy end?" His jesting was inviting but I told myself to be on guard.

"Absolutely, sir," I said. "We won't let them spoil it. And it'd be an honor to be your assistant."

"As a matter of fact, an assistant is just what I need now. Of a different sort, to be sure, but who knows where that might lead?" He looked away for a moment, nodding to the lab instructor who was just leaving. He ran his hand through his thick white hair and pulled on an earlobe, as if to clear his ear of water. I thought that might be some sort of sign, for it crossed my mind that the lab instructor might have been the woman he was with in Frankfurt the night his family was killed in the raid on Darmstadt. Very slowly he turned back toward me, and took a moment to get back to our conversation.

"Director Meyers tells me you are perhaps unhappy in your dormitory situation. Living with senior students, and so forth? Since he has made available a small house to me—you will have heard of the unfortunate circumstances I happen to find myself in—I can offer you a room of your own with separate bath facilities if you are able to take on some caretaking duties. Professional obligations force me to be away more and more, it seems. It would be prudent to have someone in the house. Alas, these days there is a lot of vandalism. And of course, since many are homeless, well … I mustn't get too graphic. I think you get the picture." He assured me that I wouldn't have to pay any rent, nothing of that sort. Since we were all, as he put it, under the same roof—courtesy of the arrangements between the TH and the American authorities.

I took a deep breath and thanked him for the offer, and he agreed to let me have a few days to think things over. He shook my hand limply and we bowed slightly to each other. After he left I watched him take Miss Mannheim, the lab instructor, who'd obviously been waiting for him, under the arm and lead her to his car at the curb. I better ask Klaus and Ingeborg for advice, I thought—for starters, assuming I decided to move out, how to explain matters to Sebastian, but especially Martin, toward whom I'd recently made a determined effort to be more open. It did occur they might be relieved to get out from under any pressures, real or imagined, to have to be nice to me.

I saw Ingeborg and Klaus later that night in a building that passed for the library. It didn't take them a minute to urge the move. Both alluded to unpleasant remarks overheard, especially between Martin and Sebastian, about their "poor Jewish cousin." Ingeborg reiterated that I should continue to give Martin the benefit of any doubt, make sure he understood that the move had nothing to do with him personally. While I had a nagging thought that I might regret being off by myself, Klaus and Ingeborg both took my hands. "We'll make sure you don't forget your student roots," Klaus said melodramatically.

"Besides," Ingeborg added, "you'll still be taking most of your meals in the *Mensa*, and we all know that's where the real action is. So you'd be foolish not to check in regularly!"

"Get your divorce over with right now!" Klaus boomed, and drew me a little map of the way back to the Quonset. "So you don't get lost on us."

Martin and Sebastian put on a pretty good show of surprise

and regret, but Sebastian added a bit too quickly that he'd be sure to forward any mail. "Speaking of which," he said, "I almost forgot. A telegram came for you a while back, sorry! Someone said you'd be gone for a while so I put it aside." He pulled it out from under his mattress. "I'm afraid the black borders mean it's grim news. Maybe that's why I filed it away without thinking. Again, I'm really sorry." My hand shook when I took it. I was sure as hell not going to open it in their presence, so I said I'd be back as soon as I had Professor Breiter's permission to move my things over. Meanwhile, Klaus suggested I just stay with him during the transition. An older student, who couldn't make it past the third week, had withdrawn.

My first impulse was not to open the telegram, ever. All I could think was, who else has gone and died? I went to the toilet. The lock on the stall was broken so I tied the door shut with my belt, needing to sit where no one could see or barge in on me. Minutes ticked by. I was growing light-headed, sitting there with the telegram on my lap, staring at the graffiti on the back of the stall's door. Finally, I managed to tear off the slightest edge and blew into the envelope. The sheet crinkled as I teased it out with a finger and let it fall, folded, onto the floor. Then I flushed the toilet several times for some loud noise. My stomach fluttered when I bent down to retrieve the telegram, spread it out on my lap, and started to read: "We regret to inform you that your grandmother has died. Her spirit remained strong to the very end. She was so grateful for your confiding in her about your deepest concerns. Now we ask you to join us in silent prayer for her soul. May God grant her peace, and you as well." It was signed by Uncle Max, who was a second father for me, in the name of the family. Tears started coming and I kept on crying till I heard a knock on the door.

"You all right in there? Need any help?" I recognized Martin's voice and asked him to give me a few more minutes. He waited patiently till I let myself out. Without a word, all I could do was hand him the telegram and take his arm. "Let's go for a little walk, shall we?" he said and I didn't have the will to object. Along the way I managed to tell him a little about Gramma. Martin just listened while guiding me along till we came to a bench on an overhang with a view of a part of town I'd not seen before. Then I lurched into some ugly curses. He looked straight ahead but seemed to listen with every fiber in his body. When I ran out of words he put his arm around my shoulder. "Just look out there," he pointed. "In a few years, if we're so fortunate, and with God's grace, everything you see that's been destroyed will be rebuilt. Life can go on if we give it the necessary boost," he said softly. "I know you'll do your part, and I'm relieved you're moving in with Breiter. It's a good move for you and I suspect for him as well. If you can't do without my company from time to time so much the better. I'm not going anywhere, either." He paused before saying my name for the first time I could recall. I started crying again, and he had the decency to walk back on his own. At dusk I put my hands on the bench and pushed myself up. It felt good to be standing again.

Changing the Subject

"Here's to none of us having flunked out!" my comrades and I kept toasting over warm beer at the local kiosk. Everyone's first-term room assignments—in Quonset huts army engineers had set up in makeshift fashion—were reconfigured to make room for incoming transfer students and new arrivals. After more beers, Martin finally pointed to Klaus, joking about how they'd likely be "ghettoized" when the authorities found out about their "non-Aryan blood." They'd just gotten word from Allied High Command, with help from the Red Cross, that due to possible Jewish ancestry they'd be allowed to file for "modest" reparations and at least continue their studies tuition-free! They stared at me for a moment, and I sensed they somehow knew I was Jewish though I'd never made a point of mentioning it or even letting it slip.

Another bombshell hit the next morning. The *TH* sent everyone a black-bordered missive that a student we didn't know, but whose heroics as a submariner were widely celebrated, had committed suicide over the weekend; and Heinz and Sebastian were asked to leave on some sort of probationary arrangement. They'd been friends of the guy, in his company of late, and apparently somehow involved. To my surprise, Martin and Klaus didn't seem curious about the details, so I wondered if they were also "involved," if more tangentially. What was clear was it was none of my business. All over campus it felt as if everyone agreed to keep the lid on, watching what one said, deferring to others. Men even held doors open for men. The sternest professors, among them Professor Breiter, went out of their way to show kindness and understanding when students slipped up.

In Breiter's case, I was especially relieved, because there were whispers I'd become his pet. Some students had seen us taking long walks in the woods south of the *TH*. He'd taken some interest in me to be sure, but I suspected it had to do with some distant American relatives who may have lived near us in Wisconsin. He'd also engaged me to house-sit on occasion when he was off lecturing elsewhere. Inasmuch as he'd lost his wife and children in the Darmstadt raid — he'd been out of town, hence escaped perishing with them — I also suspected I was substituting for his son, who'd been just about my age.

Professor Breiter returned from the first days of fall break quite alone. It was soon clear his relationship with Fräulein Mannheim, his lab assistant, was over. Once again he began inviting me to "walk around a while" several times a week, when they'd normally spend time together. He said nothing directly, but began revisiting, reliving, really, those days before the "terror attack" on Darmstadt, which everyone knew had killed his family while he was away visiting "a friend." He strained to put the matter delicately, but he could see that I knew he was mincing words. To distract him, I changed the subject somewhat, trying a few questions about his use of the expression "terror attack."

"That was a slip of my Aryan tongue," he said and I blanched. "Of course, that's what Goebbels and Goering wanted us to feel. A normal person — hah," he suddenly laughed, "as if such a person existed now — a normal person would call it an air raid, however devastating and total ..." I said nothing, and on our subsequent walk he changed the subject.

"So," he began on our last walk at the end of December before I went off on vacation, "have I not convinced you by now to make German your master, and not those wayward sciences?" He proceeded to extol my work on the *Nibelungenlied*, the centerpiece of his course, as well as encourage me to keep "fooling around" writing a few more little poems of my own in the manner of several I'd once attached to an assignment. The only professor who'd risked doing so, he recommended we all try our hand at some of our own verses to extend the epic poem, fragmented as it was.

"You obviously know your Heine," Breiter had written back. "But now's the time to enter the twentieth century. For starters, see Heym, Trakl, Dehmel, Stefan George too; then of course Benn and Rilke, as an antidote; but on your own time, not at the expense of my course!" he managed to grin.

It struck me that was way too kind. I didn't confess I was writing simple ditties to impress Miriam Pfungsheim, one of the more dazzling students in the course, on whose desk I'd drop my little forays into rhyme, absent any reason, when no one was around. At first I didn't sign them, but when I saw her looking around after she'd unfolded the slip of paper with my latest aboard, I decided to add my name to the next drop, in parentheses.

Catching sight of her looking my way at the end of class, I thought I saw a faint smile cross her lips; but that was that, so I put an end to my versifying from then on. When Breiter began to make a point of calling on me when I was sneaking glances at Miriam across the lecture hall, I suspected he suspected I was keen on her. If nothing else, he did start me revisiting my long-range plan to steer toward the sciences. At the very least, his encouragement prompted me to advance-enroll in his literature course in the spring—to ensure I'd have a place. I didn't bother finding out what it would entail, merely hoped Miriam would also be aboard.

The twice-yearly literature courses tended to be oversubscribed, which people like Director Meyers, as well as the supervising American authorities, took as a sign students wanted to look into the mirror of fictional worlds by way of a deeper understanding of themselves, as the position paper argued. Director Meyers was said to be petitioning to add several more such courses to what was substantially a science curriculum, while his antagonists pointed to the road leading to the Pedagogical Institute in a nearby village, saying in effect, "Go south if you want that sort of education!" — minor clearly implied.

On a dark, snowy night late in December, shortly before we'd split for the holidays, Klaus mentioned almost in passing his desire to turn to language teaching as a way to help the young get off to a start that would never again result "in their being bamboozled by devils who pervert language into a deadly weapon." We were lazily cleaning out our quarters, getting ready to move at the beginning of the new term, when Klaus also confided he'd not be around much in the spring since he was transitioning to a transfer — "I'm taking that road south, but if you get me a buddy-pass I'll be happy to join you in the showers at the Officers' Club in Darmstadt," he said, jabbing my chin playfully. When anyone found out I was able to enjoy a hot shower there from time to time, the teasing rained down on me.

"You'd never clear security with all your Jewish blood," I jabbed back. "Martin might, with his thimbleful." I ran like hell out the door. He'd begun throwing books after me.

Just before I was off to Tuttlingen, where I'd been invited to spend breaks by the Kramers, relatives of family friends, the mailman delivered what was the smallest envelope the post allowed. It was decorated with odd little flowers and insects, and I could just make out the postmark, from a town I couldn't place. When I flipped it over to the return address, I finally made the leap: Miriam Pfungsheim, c/o *Die Waldorfschule*.

"Dear Mr. American Exchange Student," she began, "suspect you're wondering why I'm not back at the *TH* where I trust this finds you." While I'd not forgotten her, it took me a moment to conjure her up again in my mind's eye, because she was strangely absent after mid-terms. "Well, my old teacher," the note continued, "whom I've been assisting in a sort of practicum-exercise since mid-term (to see if elementary education's for me) suddenly took ill just before I was set to return to the *TH*, and the school here was quite desperate to engage me to fill in for the remainder of the term, which I'm still sort of digesting. Of course, it wouldn't have been possible without Director Meyer's support, who in his typical way said he couldn't imagine a more important mission. So he's arranged for a temporary leave, which I understand is highly unusual. You can imagine I feel some pressure to do a decent job. After all, in effect I'm not going to have to finish my courses; though I'm still obliged to make up the exams, which'll probably be the end of me, but still …

"Anyway, what I'm trying to say is I've taken your verses with me in a little box. Every time I open it, read through them again, I'm cheered by their mix of serious and silly, so I just wanted to let you know your poetic beginnings are available for your future biographer! Let's have a cup of whatever when I return at the end of spring term. Meanwhile, the children I'm working with also like to write little verses, as well as express themselves artistically with colored pencils. Quite graphically expressed, don't you think, by their drawings on the envelope? Thinking of you, best wishes, Miriam P."

"So, exactly how beautiful is she?" Klaus said to Martin more than to me when they caught me standing there fingering the little envelope, staring into space in something of a trance.

"Anyone we should know?" Martin baited me. When I stiffened, closed one eye, and kissed the envelope tenderly,

Martin shouted, "Step right up, folks. What we have here is a lovesick freak, who'll amaze you with feats of ... Well, hurry now, get your tickets for a seat inside the tent!" Holding out my arms as a sleepwalker might, I took some monster steps straight out of *Frankenstein*, and was about to clobber them when they hightailed it back to the Quonsets.

"Time for a full confession," Martin said when we met later for a bratwurst and beer at the corner kiosk. "Klaus has put the kibosh on me. I'm deserting you too, pal. But now that Heinz and Sebastian are gone off to their private hells, you won't need much protection from your one-thirty-second Jewish bodyguards. Besides, there's a higher good at work here, so cut the moping, pay attention!"

Klaus cut in, "We're going to do our utmost to revolutionize education in the Motherland. Assuming we get our teaching certificates, we're going to steal some ideas from Minna Specht and her *Waldorfschule*, do background work in Pestalozzi and Montessori, throw in some Uncle Freud; and what the hell, even come to live off you in the States awhile to see what folks like John Dewey are up to. Eventually, the goal's to open up our own private school, maybe on an island in the North Sea, one the Nazis didn't sink. Or die trying. We hope someone's told you along the way to expect to pay back our hospitality. Like a good Greek Jew ..." At the mention of the *Waldorfschule*, I decided to keep Miriam's note a secret. I knew Klaus was constantly on the lookout for female companionship, to put it politely; and he'd taken an interest in my interest in her. But I pledged my general allegiance, which Martin said he hoped meant real dollars down the road. We drank to money, lots of it. They both said they'd have me over to their new digs when they'd settled into the "castle" the Pedagogical Institute was housed in. It had been spared during the war, thanks in part to an enormous red cross painted on the roof; more likely, however, because it had been in the Mountbatten family for years; a.k.a. the Battenbergs, generations removed.

Klaus and Martin gave me the finger when I suggested they were really bailing out to escape Quonset life. "And what'll you do when winter really batters us? When the wind stops at paned windows, doesn't blow notes and papers into the hallway? Or worse, freeze your hair you've just washed in nice icy water?" I yelled after them, before I had the good sense to say a prayer for their being in the world at all, and a big part of mine to boot.

End-of-term exams had come and gone. While I wouldn't have won high honors or anything close if there had been such distinctions, I didn't embarrass my professors, as the director put it when I stopped by to wish him and his family happy holidays. He took a moment to recall a high point: my failure to name the most prominent mathematician working in the "new" Germany at the moment. When I hemmed and hawed, Professor Thyen, one of my three examiners, whispered, "He's sitting right before you, son ..."

Quickly changing the subject after we joined in for a laugh, I asked after the director's son, wondering why I hadn't seen little Rupert around much of late. He'd sometimes sneak into my Quonset to ask about America, obviously his major fantasy-land, especially when it came to Cowboys and Indians. To my relief, I learned Rupert was feeling himself again and off on an extended vacation visiting an aunt in Kiel who kept horses, and Rupert was delighted at the prospect of grooming them.

"I'm afraid he'll come back sick again as he usually does travelling and all," the director let slip. When I whispered I'd bump Rupert up the prayer list—our family's mantra—it was clear that was too much information so I quickly took my leave.

Before catching the train for Tuttlingen, I made the rounds of Professor Breiter's house and grounds one last time, checking the notepad by the phone where he usually left last-minute instructions to see to this or that. In his large scrawl with the laundry marker he liked to use, he left a cheery note about how well I'd done on the *Nibelungenlied* exam; having chosen the striking option everyone else had shied away from, he wrote, and that alone was "quite commendable." He voiced great surprise (a compliment?) at the "ease" with which I'd produced the ten additional stanzas to the *Nibelungenlied* the exam called for: "in a manner concurrent and congruous with the unfinished ending of the text."

Checking the grandfather clock on the professor's mantle so I wouldn't be late for the train I knew would leave the very minute the station clock struck ten, I noticed to my great shock it was stuck on 9:19, the very minute, I recalled, the first bombs fell in the most devastating raid on Darmstadt, the night of 11 September, 1944 — the professor's way of memorializing his family who'd perished.

Hurrying down the cobbly path for the tram to the railroad station, stones flying underfoot, I didn't look around until I was sitting in the third-class compartment of the express, bracing myself on the splintered wooden bench.

It Takes All Kinds

My first semester over at the *TH*, I decided to try to visit the Kramers during the semester break. Sybille Kramer was the sister of my gramma's dear friend back in the States, and she and her husband Richard wrote they'd be "honored" if I could spend any holiday time with them at their "modest little abode" in Tuttlingen, a small town in Swabia, through which the baby Danube ran. They'd lived there for many years and somehow survived the war, though Mrs. Kramer was Jewish. I'd been warned not to go near that subject if I ever visited them.

After some delay in the phone system badly disjointed by the war, an operator connected us. Mrs. Kramer and I were equally surprised to hear each other's voices. Hers was couched in pretty standard High German with no trace of a Swabian accent I'd been warned to expect. She sounded quite excited at the prospect of my coming. "The sooner the sooner," she said with genuine warmth. We agreed on the day after tomorrow so they could take care of little things, prepare my quarters properly, and I'd have a chance to gather my stuff together for the journey.

"My husband will meet you at the station. Only one train comes from Stuttgart at that hour so not to worry, they're won't be any chance of a mix-up. Richard, I should warn you, will arrive on his pet motorcycle and look quite imposing in his goggles, not to mention World War I leather flyer's helmet. It's a big machine so he can easily tie your belongings on behind you. You'll still have plenty of room to enjoy the ride back to our house. Just be sure to hang on tight! He's something of a menace, but the French police just stop traffic and wave him right through," she laughed.

"The French police?"

"Yes, dear boy. We rejoice we're in The French Zone. Many of our friends are in the occupying business and are also looking forward to meeting you. You may be their first American who is not in uniform. So *ta ta* now, have a safe journey and don't forget to enjoy the drama of the Black Forest on the way down. But I beg you: we have plenty of cuckoo clocks so please resist bringing us one as a gift! Oh, I almost forgot, there's one bridge you cross that will make your heart skip if you look down. But we're told it has been inspected and remains entirely safe. The Nazis never got around to blowing it up." She hung up with a soft click before I could say anything else. From the brief exchange, I thought if Richard were anything at all like his wife I'd be right at ease.

I made sure I was at the station in plenty of time for the morning express to Stuttgart because I was traveling third class, no reservation, and wanted to grab a window seat. I'd forgotten that third-class compartments had wooden benches: the seat I hurriedly slid into was splintered. What did Gramma used to say? Something about traveling with sandpaper for life's rough edges … The compartment filled quickly, and I opened the window for air. Though the little plaque nailed to the window warned, "Do Not Lean Out," I promptly did. People on the platform, waiting for the local, were sitting on their suitcases, wiping sweat off their weary faces, gulping down drinks. Fellow travelers who'd entered behind me were already breaking out sandwiches. I'd forgotten about food altogether and tried disguising my sudden hunger. An old man unwrapped a newspaper, tore a sausage free of the links that fell out, and handed it to me.

"Sorry," he said, "there's no mustard."

"Well, next time see that there is!" I risked saying, nibbling at it gingerly, relieved he began shrugging his shoulders, laughing.

Our little joke went over badly with a woman who whispered

to her companion behind a gloved hand, but loud enough for me to hear, something about "the young having lost all respect." The old man merely closed his eyes and promptly took a nap.

Heidelberg was our first stop. We crossed the Neckar River in light mist and the storied hill on its north side, the *Philosophenweg*—where famous minds were said to have argued serious matters, sometimes coming to blows, even duels—was nothing more than a soft charcoal line in an artist's sketch. Beneath us, running to join the Rhine to the west, the Neckar seemed coated in oil slicks from the coal barges lumbering by. A lone woman on the back deck of a tug looked up from hanging wash on a line. I couldn't get the window down in time to wave, which relieved the women in our compartment who'd continued their whispering.

From the station, I made out the flying buttresses and gargoyles hanging down imposingly from the famous medieval castle overlooking the river from the south bank. In what was turning out to be my favorite course—the one humanities course we science majors were obliged to enroll in—Professor Breiter had mentioned the Nibelungs' presence all over this landscape, tracing their peregrinations on an old map he'd managed to salvage somewhere—"like Indian tribes in your West, albeit even more ferocious," he'd said.

Some verses of the text came to mind so I took out a pad and began scanning them when the old man, suddenly jolted awake, poked me with his umbrella: "You ought to use our stop-over here to put your feet on holy ground, young man." He took my pad and scribbled his address on it. "Next time I'll put you up, serve you my best mustard. Meanwhile, my regards to your people in America. If they rent you out as a grandson I will be happy to negotiate a visit. My only grandson, you see, was killed in the damnable war." He put his hand down hard on my shoulder and squeezed.

I forced the window open to watch him slowly make his way to the exit, several times doffing his cap at passing ladies. The train started up just as I hailed a vendor, and hastily got myself a bottle of lemonade he thrust through the window. Finally, the conductor came along, which started up a heated discussion over the train's continuing route by the women across from me. Perking up, because I was suddenly confused about the next stretch, I leaned their way a little. It seems the train was about to be rerouted over Karlsruhe, not proceed directly on to Stuttgart. The women began protesting that "such shenanigans" wouldn't have been tolerated in The Third Reich, and furthermore, that we were already running some minutes late. "It is such a scandal," the older woman spit out, but no one except her companion joined in. I myself wondered if the route change meant I'd miss my connection to Tuttlingen, assuming we made it to Stuttgart at all.

"Well, nothing's guaranteed anymore, that I do know," the conductor said. "But I will try to find out just how late we might be into Stuttgart, my good man." He punched my ticket and left.

Rumors started flying up and down the whole car: we were transporting lawyers and judges to the newly-constituted German Supreme Court, to be situated in Karlsruhe; the tracks had given out south of Heidelberg due to negligence; the Americans were sending through a secret shipment of Nazi gold to Swiss banks ... Exasperated, the older woman looked my way and said, "Why doesn't our *Ami* here just drop another atomic bomb and put us out of our misery?"

Chanting verses from the *Nibelungenlied* I'd been reviewing back at her, I toasted her with my lemonade for good measure. She grunted something about my impertinent impudence, but when she jumped up to retrieve her belongings from the rack overhead I beat her to them. I took the bundles and suitcases down, hers and then her companion's, who also pointed to a lampshade—"Please, this also," she scowled—and, politely as I could, helped them into the aisle where they proceeded to push through the car and finally out of sight. The three other people in the compartment settled back, stretched out, and the man with one arm carefully unwrapped a bar of chocolate and gave me a chunk.

"Takes all kinds, you understand," he said.

"Sure enough," I said, relieved. "Where are you headed, may I ask?"

"Well, I'm sort of a refugee myself," he said plaintively, "but maybe my sister in Karlsruhe will put me up for a while till I can decide some things." He paused to wolf down the rest of the chocolate bar before carefully pressing out the wrapper on his knee and returning it to his pocket. "Before the war, I'd been learning the machine tool trade, but with this gone"—he pointed to the stump of his arm—"well, I'm open to suggestions if you have any." I shook my head slowly and told him a little about my circumstances. Thinking I'd doze off a little to fend off my anxiety about making the Stuttgart connection, I let slip that I was more or less a student at the *Technische Hochschule*. He sat up abruptly.

"Holy Mother of God!" he said. "What a bloodbath!" The Heidelberg newspaper he pulled out of his rucksack had the story splashed on the front page. "Don't suppose you care to read about the latest developments?"

A few days before the semester ended, a student had been found murdered on the back side of Darmstadt, and the grisly details were starting to leak out. For some students, particularly those who'd fought on the Russian front and somehow survived, it was just another death they seemed to be able to shrug off. Everyone passed the many editions of the *Echo* around, the local paper, but it was clear the investigation would take a long time so most of us stopped waiting for the next edition and went back to our studies.

"Not hardly" I said softly, and gently pushed his newspaper aside. "Think I better get some rest now." Closing my eyes, I prayed I'd really fall asleep. I could see, before slipping under, that he went back to the paper, running a finger under some bit or other. When we ground to a stop at Karlsruhe, I jumped up, sweating and chilled. My chocolate provider had already moved to the rear of the car to get off. The whole compartment was empty, and I thought I might have it all to myself for the zag back east, then across and down toward Stuttgart, when I heard the conductor shouting.

"All out for Stuttgart! This train is being held over in Karlsruhe. Hurry to Track 4, use the underpass, and please see you take all your belongings." He assured me when I met him on the platform that we'd make up the lost time. I'd not only make my connection, but the new train would continue on to Tuttlingen so there'd be no need to change trains again. "In the new Germany you will be in Tuttlingen," he thumbed the timetable, "at exactly the same time you'd have arrived in the old." The train on Track 4 started whistling, so I quickly thanked him and bolted. In short order I found an empty compartment, relieved to be able to stay put all the way to Tuttlingen.

Stuttgart came and went with no disasters. Spookily, no one else joined me for the last leg. I could pace around the compartment to stretch, get the buzz out of my legs at any time. The landscape began rushing by the window the harder I strained to stare out.

Early evening came on, and I hoped for enough light to see what Mrs. Kramer had promised would be the most beautiful part of the journey — through deepening valleys, along pristine streams, under and over gracefully arcing spans, a final cut through the heart of the Black Forest, then on into sleepy little

Tuttlingen with its umbrella of red-slate rooftops. I dreamt the final stretch, wondering how anyone living in such a landscape could have ever dreamt of ...

Assumptions

Not an hour's drive north of Lake Constance, blanketed by red-tile roofs as far as the eye can see, Tuttlingen nestles in a lazy valley south of the Black Forest, through which the baby Danube trickles. The Kramer's little stucco house on *Uhlandstraße* would, I hoped, eventually become a home away from home.

Living a virtual fairy tale existence the first week, pampered as I'd only been by my Gramma, I was suddenly jolted awake by a letter that arrived just days before I was set to return to my studies. From Ingeborg Steinbach's sister, in prose that made me shiver, I read that Ingeborg had suffered something of a "nervous breakdown" and was spirited to a psychiatric clinic outside Meersburg on Lake Constance, not far from Tuttlingen! It seems she had been having dark dreams about her beloved twin brother, Uwe, whose submarine never returned from a mission to test the British blockade of a North Sea port, and so she was unable to keep up with her studies. Though he'd been ill and hence hadn't been aboard for the fateful mission, she continued to dream him dead on occasion.

Ever sensitive to others' plights, the Kramers immediately offered to drive me to the clinic. Only later did I learn Sybille had also been treated there, as a result of her own traumatic time during the war. A lapsed Catholic, Richard had had to hide Sybille on a remote farm because she was Jewish. Unlike Sadie, Sybille's twin, who'd fled Germany just in time, the Kramers thought things would never get "that bad," as indeed so many other German Jews had.

Sybille called ahead to the clinic, was told we could visit the very next day, and to check in at the reception desk. We arrived and were approved to see Ingeborg but were told we'd have to wait a bit for her to recover from what we learned later was yet another shock treatment. Rather than join me, Sybille said they'd stroll around the grounds with her little dachshund Waldi in tow. "No hurry. I want to retrace some steps I took here in 1946 when they saved me from myself," she said darkly.

Richard helped her past the moment. "We'll be happy to meet Miss Steinbach after you've visited," he said.

Following a nurse to the sunroom, I was startled to see Ingeborg sprawled out on a divan, her arms stretched out overhead. "It's to work out the kinks in my shoulders," she said matter-of-factly, as if we'd just met for coffee in the *TH*'s little snack bar. Her hair, usually braided atop her head like a tiara, hung lank and seemed unwashed. The cord to her wrap-around gray gown was knotted in several places. When I tried making eye contact, she suddenly shielded her eyes. It was clear she didn't want to talk "school stuff," so I told her a little about life with the Kramers. As soon as I began asking her about life at the clinic, I realized it was a mistake. All she said was, "You don't want to know," after which we exchanged a few glances between staring down at the floor or out the window. Just then I caught sight of the Kramers and waved them in.

After perfunctory introductions, Sybille asked Ingeborg if she'd like to take a little ferry ride across Lake Constance. Richard said he was pretty sure the ferry was still running; they hadn't taken it across to Switzerland and back for some time, and Waldi liked the lake's breezes. Waldi barked and Ingeborg shared in our laugh. She bent down and as if on command Waldi sprang into her arms. Rubbing his ears, stroking his head, she said, "I think I would like such a nice little outing, but first you must get my doctor's approval, yes?" Richard was quick to nod, headed for the reception desk to inquire, and we were soon led to her psychiatrist's office.

Dr. Meinholtz pulled three chairs together for us, another to his side for Ingeborg. After some small talk he turned to Ingeborg, pushed his horn-rimmed glasses up his forehead and said, "Well, Ingeborg, would you like that?"

Ingeborg put her hands in her lap and bent over to stare at her shoes. "I think I would like to see Switzerland for the first time in my life."

"Well, that settles it, my friends. All we must insist on is you have Ingeborg back in time for bed at 10:00 PM. I believe the last ferry docks back in Meersburg at 9:00 PM so there shouldn't be a problem. I'll have my secretary call for the schedule to make sure." He exchanged bows with Richard, shook hands all around, and asked his nurse to see about a change of clothes for Ingeborg, who bounced along after her.

There was space on the back deck for only six cars, which were driven aboard before we were allowed to follow. When a deckhand removed the rope, calling out "please, each person must have a ticket to present," Sybille hurriedly handed me two. I had to open Ingeborg's hand to position her fingers around the ticket while repeating the deckhand's instructions in her ear. She suddenly seemed too excited to pay attention. My feet buzzing under me, I felt nauseated. Richard put a comforting hand on my shoulder, "Courage. We'll be fine as soon as we push off. But let's hurry to the lounge for a table. Take Waldi and grab one. Sybille and I will bring Ingeborg with us." The crowd began surging ahead, and like a runner at the start of a race I braced myself for the signal to come aboard.

Seated in the lounge, we looked out a broad picture window that a deckhand had just squeegeed clean, and watched the crew prepare the boat for departure. A voice over the loudspeaker emphasized that we'd have exactly ninety minutes' shore-time in Romanshorn. The return trip would not be delayed for any stragglers; the company could not be responsible for anyone who failed to show up exactly on time, the voice added sternly. "If I hear the word 'exactly' one more time," Richard growled. "Well, never mind."

Richard ordered some coffee for us from the steward moving among the tables. Sybille chastised him when Ingeborg said that she couldn't tolerate coffee, must have tea instead, the steward long since having disappeared into the galley. "Okay, sorry," Richard said meekly. "Sybille's quite right. I should not make assumptions. Forgive me, Miss Steinbach, I should have asked you first."

With that he went looking for the steward. Ingeborg suddenly started fidgeting in her chair, then grew noticeably anxious, mumbling something about being so uncomfortable. We tried offering her our chairs, but she stood up and trotted over to another table. We could hear her asking the young couple if they'd mind giving up a third chair, which she tried out with some pomp in their presence. Sybille coughed nervously. I bumped Waldi under his chin with my foot, immediately regretting it because he took off after Richard in the vicinity of the galley. Before I could make a move to run after him, Ingeborg jumped up and gave chase, as if to say, "I'll find him, don't worry." She even smiled back at us before she rounded a corner.

When Richard finally returned, Waldi tucked under his arm, Ingeborg was not with them. Indeed, Richard was surprised to learn she'd followed him into the passageway. We looked at one another, suddenly quite uneasy about Ingeborg's disappearance. Meanwhile, the turbines started turning over. We could see the crew struggling to loosen huge ropes holding us fast, then heave them toward workers on the dock. People on shore began waving as we backed out of the slip and arced around the harbor's jetties.

Trying to pretend at first that all was normal, we drank our coffee in silence, Richard opening a magazine of Romanshorn's sights he'd picked up somewhere. He started to read, though it was clear he was as worried as Sybille and I. At our feet, Waldi seemed anxious as well. "If only you were a bloodhound," Richard said, "you could make yourself useful for a change." Waldi whimpered as if to agree.

"Let's wait another fifteen minutes or so," Sybille finally suggested, "before we split up to look for her. It's not that big a boat, she should be easy to locate somewhere." And call for help, I thought to myself. Unable to concentrate on reading, Richard laid the magazine aside and took out fifteen matches from a tiny tin, which he always seemed to carry around to torment me with his maddening little game. With his thick fingers he spread them out on the table, like little wooden soldiers with red faces, I couldn't help thinking. As he always did to entice me, he said I could have the first move.

"Richard, my head aches just thinking about all the options and combinations. Besides, if you'd just let me win for once, you'd have yourself a more willing victim." He threw up his hands in mock disgust and promptly challenged himself to a game.

"Okay, time's up," Sybille said. "Since there are three decks, let's each take one and meet back here in half an hour. With Ingeborg!" she added, as if to ensure our finding her. "And I'm now just deciding: Richard, you cover the deck below, I'll take this one, and you," she turned to me, "get to climb up top for a look." The ferry had worked its way out into open waters. People were beginning to leave the lounge to stroll around on deck, so we entered the stream after synchronizing our watches.

Up on the top deck, I even opened the large bins where life boats were stored, looking as well under the canvas covering the lifeboats. No trace of her at all, so I turned in desperation to a ship's officer I came across. He couldn't recall seeing the person I described. "I'm sure she'll turn up, or find you by the time we dock. It's not as if we're on the Prinzessin Eugenia, our much larger sister ship," he said so matter-of-factly I calmed down some. I considered retracing my steps in the few minutes left till we'd agreed to meet back in the lounge. Starting back down the steps to the middle deck, staring out for a moment at the lake, I realized the one place I hadn't searched were the waters around us!

I'd have made a poor look-out because my eyes couldn't discern much of anything besides sunlight all over the surface and lots of little waves going one way, then back another, when smaller craft crisscrossed behind and ahead of us. If only Richard had his binoculars along, I thought, until I recalled the trouble I'd had looking for signs of wild boar on a hunt he'd taken me on north of Tuttlingen. Trying not to panic — I couldn't imagine what would happen if we alerted the crew about a person possibly having gone overboard — I started running to the lounge. There I found Richard drumming his fingers on the table, while Waldi lapped water from a bowl at his feet.

"No luck in your assigned bailiwick either, I see," he said. "Might as well get some sun and breeze while we're waiting." The doors to the outside deck were roped open so we stepped to the railing, leaning into the wind. Richard asked me to cup my hands so he could light up the remains of the cigar he'd tortured back at the clinic. "Sybille will see us out here, or Waldi will let her know." He hadn't protested being left tied to the table. I'd almost forgotten we were supposed to be on a nice little outing and looked up at the huge sky. Behind us, Meersburg was fading fast into some mist. When I directed Richard's attention to the horizon ahead and said I could make out Swiss hills, if faintly, he gave me a playful shove as if to push me overboard.

ASSUMPTIONS

"That's a mirage. We won't see land for another half hour or so, it's just too foggy. Hey, look at that bird just off the stern! Might be an egret, definitely not a ubiquitous gull—unless it's that stupid brown gull on the pier Ingeborg couldn't fatten up with the rest of her sandwich." Richard winced when he caught himself saying her name. "Hope that doesn't jinx anything," he said at last.

We were starting to relax a bit when a stewardess came up. Confirming we were the Kramers, she said she'd been sent by Sybille to tell us that both our "womenfolk" were delayed in the restroom on the lower deck. They would look for us in the lounge by and by. Richard tried tipping her but she backed off, slightly offended.

"Well," he threw the butt he was smoking over the side, "this calls for a brand new cigar." I said I'd rather just have more coffee. "Okay, but how about that game now?" he said, as we sat back down in the lounge and ordered. Of course he won for the umpteenth time but, laughing his deep laugh, promised he'd show me the trick to the strategy when I next passed through Tuttlingen. When Sybille and Ingeborg failed to show up at all, our mood turned sour again.

As we approached the harbor at Romanshorn, Sybille finally appeared, huffing and puffing, quite alone. Hurriedly she explained that Ingeborg had had to lie down in the nurse's station—there was no doctor aboard so all she was given was aspirin. Sybille said it was best we go ashore and have a bite to eat, at which time she'd recount what had happened—she was simply too upset to say anything else for now. Inasmuch as we were about to dock and the loudspeaker began barking instructions about disembarkation procedures, Sybille said above the din and bustle, "Remember 'Hope is patience with the lamp burning'— some ancient Roman's apt way with a phrase. I said I'll tell you what I can when we're in some quiet corner of a restaurant."

We were finally waved ashore, again with the reminder to return in exactly ninety minutes. Marching to the first restaurant we found, we didn't look around at the town, or even the menu framed on the door. The hostess gave us a choice of tables, leading us to one Richard pointed to, off by itself at the rear near the kitchen. Waldi jumped up on the fourth chair and no one seemed to mind, while Sybille slumped back, trying to find words for what she'd witnessed. She'd had an immediate instinct to head for the women's restroom first, guessing Ingeborg might have taken ill or needed to splash some water on her face. Nothing darker. Sure enough, she was in a stall, but sobbing uncontrollably. Asking another woman present to keep watch outside and reroute others to other facilities, Sybille wanted time alone with Ingeborg to sort things out. As soon as Sybille identified herself, Ingeborg calmed down, but soon she began slamming her fists against the sides of the stall, yelling things Sybille couldn't quite comprehend, except for Ingeborg repeating a name sounding like Uwe over and over. Eventually, Ingeborg ran out of steam, muffling her sobs into agonizing sighs. Finally, she simply fell silent altogether.

"I was just telling her, over and over, that I wasn't going to leave her, that I'd be there no matter what, and please to take her time to come back to herself," Sybille said. When the waiter finished serving our soup, which is all we wanted, Richard didn't even order a beer, his usual drink at meals. I passed the rolls, waiting for Sybille to continue when she could.

Breaking a roll to feed to Waldi, Sybille took a moment to say, "Ingeborg finally unlocked the door after I asked her to, and like a submissive child let me lead her to the nurse's station I'd noticed along the way. I hoped they'd have something to sedate her. As I said earlier, all they had was some aspirin—quite astonishing if you think about it. Well, when she swallowed two tablets, she closed her eyes and seemed to want to sleep, so the nurse and I stepped outside. We debated calling the clinic for advice." Sybille fed Waldi more bread before going on. "Now I think we'd best just keep her as quiet and calm as possible till we can get her back to Meersburg. In the meantime, just be with her, not say anything much if at all, unless she does." Sybille looked at Waldi as if to say, "Any other ideas, boy?" Then she pushed her soup away. Richard waved for the check. We hurried back to the ferry in silence, Waldi leading the way.

A block from the dock we could make out frantic waves from the nurse, in her bright white uniform, high up on the wheel-deck, and an officer running toward us, shouting. Out of breath, Sybille and Richard had to stop a moment, so Waldi and I raced to meet him halfway. To judge from his eyes, he seemed as frightened as we were but wouldn't say anything till the Kramers caught up. And then only would we "please proceed straight to the captain's quarters to hear what had happened," as he wasn't authorized to say anything.

"You mean," Richard forced out, "that couldn't be held against your company? Isn't that right, sailor?"

"Richard, please," Sybille implored, fanning herself with her little purse while quickening her steps to keep up. "This good man's doing his best. Let's just pray that Ingeborg's …" She was unable to finish her thought. Richard and I took her under the arms, helping her up the gangplank, the captain and nurse looking down from above. The officer accompanying us offered to mind Waldi while we went ahead but Waldi growled his best. "You don't have to plead your case—you're in this with us, my pet," Sybille said.

The captain showed us to his cabin, the nurse at his side, pale, her cheek twitching. The captain, whose adjutant joined us, made a point of pulling out his own desk chair for Sybille, while Richard and I stood, Waldi curled around our feet. The nurse, hands behind her back, braced against the door. Slowly folding his hands when he and his adjutant had also taken a seat, the captain asked the nurse to give us an exact account of what had happened after we left the boat. "Please feel free to correct yourself if you suddenly recall anything else while making your report," he said to her before instructing his adjutant to take careful notes of what he called, hesitating, "only an initial, informal hearing."

We were shaken to learn that when the nurse left Ingeborg alone briefly to get her some nourishment, as she put it, and returned "really right away," Ingeborg had simply vanished. No one saw her from that moment forward. While the whole boat was undergoing a search, a vigorous attempt had been made to comb the dock area as well. Everyone encountered was asked if they'd seen someone of her description. Another passenger, someone with "a good pencil," had even drawn a little portrait of Ingeborg based on the nurse's recollection of her features, which was shown to all interviewed, on deck as well as ashore.

When the nurse finished, obviously strung out by "the worst nightmare" of her professional life, the captain took a moment to console her. Then he told us in graver tones that a boat had been lowered to search the surrounding waters, which the harbor police, also immediately alerted, had now joined. Company officials had also been notified and stood by to offer any help requested. Every aspect of the investigation was now under the jurisdiction of the gendarmerie of Romanshorn, since Ingeborg disappeared while the ferry was in port. After the captain gave us a while to collect ourselves, he said we'd be obliged to be driven to police headquarters for a further exchange of information. "Of course," he finished up, "we will not be going anywhere until my ship has been cleared for departure by the authorities. There's no telling how long that might involve, so all returning passengers will be given free lodging for the night in local accommodations if we're delayed past midnight. No boats the size of ours are allowed to cross the lake later than that."

We couldn't see ourselves waiting till morning if there were any chance we'd be cleared by midnight, so we told him he could count on at least four return-passengers. "Three humans, one part-human," Richard cracked, looking down at Waldi.

When we reached the police station, we asked the detective in charge to call the Meersburg clinic as soon as possible. He got an immediate connection. After identifying himself to Dr. Meinholtz's satisfaction, he sketched in what was known so far about "this most unfortunate situation." Then he handed the phone promptly to Sybille. One could see he was relieved to have her finish with the doctor. The most acutely verbal of us, she cut through to what our role should be now, and didn't waste time on extended excuses or apologies. Besides, it was apparent from listening to her respond to the doctor that, legally speaking, the clinic would have to assume entire responsibility.

"Only Sybille," Richard whispered, with love for her written all over him, "could have survived those terrible war years in the loft on that farm."

He didn't have to pump up my admiration, though I listened to her intensity and focus with amazement, as did the detective, who said when she handed the phone back, "We could use someone like you around here, dear lady!"

While the detective reviewed a few more details with Ingeborg's doctor, tapping his pencil absentmindedly, rolling his eyes from time to time, Sybille patted my hand, anticipating what was welling up in me. Suddenly, I started crying and couldn't stop. "Not being able to do anything," she said soothingly, "is often the worst. Besides, before I forget, Dr. Meinholtz will notify Ingeborg's sister right away. And he was also quite reassuring. Apparently this sort of thing can and does happen when patients are approved for little outings, especially those undergoing shock treatments. But they haven't lost one yet, he said, which didn't exactly amuse me. Still ... Let's all step back from these feelings we're all feeling, overwhelming as they are. Just remember, it's really not our responsibility to make things right—right now, anyway. At least I refuse to take on any more guilt at this time in my life." She tapped me lightly on the hand with Waldi's leash. "Here, a little walk will do you both some good. Richard will sit with me till we're excused."

"Sorry, ma'am," the detective said in between last words over the phone, motioning me to remain. Talk about naïve, or just plain stupid: it hadn't occurred that I was something of a material witness. I knew more about Ingeborg than anyone present so for the next hour or so, with a secretary taking notes, the detective asked me to tell them anything and everything I possibly could. "And please don't edit yourself," he added. "Something you think trivial might be a key. And another thing, young fellow, while I appreciate your speaking German, perhaps you wouldn't feel demoted by resorting to English when you can't be exact or precise enough in German? Please not to take offense!"

I was taken aback, because I'd not used English for so long that when I wrote home recently it felt really strange. Swallowing hard, I managed to promise I'd use English in a pinch before plowing ahead in German, dredging up everything I could think of Ingeborg's words and ways. Finally, I was released. However, before we could all leave, he wanted to see Sybille and the nurse alone one last time, to make sure, since they'd last been with Ingeborg, that nothing had been overlooked. Richard and I agreed he seemed a good man for the job, as we waited outside with a crewman who'd been assigned to drive us back to the ferry to wait aboard for word of whether or not we'd sail that night.

The nurse sought us out, suggesting we might like to rest a little. "I'm certain the captain will let you use his private quarters, where we store additional cots," she thought.

We must have been cleared to sail at some point, because

none of us stirred till very early the next morning and realized we'd long since docked back in Meersburg. Even Waldi must have gone into the same deep sleep. Richard had to rouse him. "Let's get some breakfast," he said, "then stop by the clinic before heading back to Tuttlingen. My foreman's either got the garage running smoothly, even thinking he might have already inherited it; or he's soused somewhere, thinking—well, who knows what his crazy mind might be entertaining." Richard, Sybille had said at one point, is a saint for having put up with Hermann, his foreman, over the years.

As soon as we arrived at the clinic we were ushered into Dr. Meinholtz's office. He was enormously relieved to impart that Ingeborg was safe in St. Gallen, where she was a guest of the "famous' monastery," which is known for taking in lost souls of all sorts. Home of so many ancient and medieval treasures, he was pleased to add. "Somehow she managed to hitchhike there with a friendly trucker, who saw her standing so close to the road he had to swerve to avoid hitting her. Just how she eluded you all and got that far we shall probably never know. But at least she's in excellent hands for now."

He played with his monocle and took a moment to scratch Waldi's back, which got so noticeably on Sybille's nerves that Dr. Meinholtz realized he'd better continue his account. "Actually, the trucker couldn't be sure she was really hitchhiking, since she seemed dazed," he went on, "but at least she didn't resist his invitation to ride along on his run to St. Gallen. Fortuitously, inasmuch as the good man was delivering supplies to the monastery's kitchen, he promptly turned her over to the monk in charge. She didn't resist, and thank goodness she was able to make clear she had a sister in Darmstadt. That's where things stand for now. Her sister is this morning on her way to St. Gallen. So far as we know she is planning to bring Ingeborg back here so we can put our heads together about how to proceed with her treatment. That pretty much sums things up for now, but perhaps you have some questions at this juncture?" Sybille, then Richard and I shook our heads, Waldi started barking as if he'd never barked before, and we left.

"I think we all need a vacation now," Richard said, starting up the car. "But not in St. Gallen!"

Burying Beetles

THE Kramer's stucco house on the Uhlandstraße had become a home away from home. Fortune would have it that I'd studied Uhland's poetry in one of my required German courses, so that was a bonus. Inasmuch as we'd run out of time for me to answer all the Kramer's questions in the fall, during the Christmas break I came prepared to offer more detail, especially how I'd managed to earn a fellowship to further my scientific education in Germany, and what my plans were for the future. Childless, the Kramers would sometimes joke they were interested in adopting me, Richard playfully pulling my ear, Sybille tousling my hair, while their dachshund Waldi ran circles around us, barking his little head off.

Huddled in their Daimler alongside the station where they'd taken me to collect a trunk I'd shipped ahead, stuffed with gifts for them my parents had sent, and a number of rubber bones for Waldi, I was still processing learning that Sybille, a "Jewess," had to be hidden on a nearby farm during the war. It was looked after by Hedwig Braunfel, who had risked her life fashioning a false loft in the barn for Sybille, as well as helping Richard bury the Daimler in the farm's well, to keep them both out of the hands of the Nazis. Provided Sybille agreed—so far she was reluctant to—Richard said he'd try to arrange a visit so I could see what Sybille had had to endure, as well as meet Hedwig, "a veritable heroine," they both sang.

Even Waldi was bundled up against the sudden inclement weather. He and Sybille nestled in the back seat, while Richard scraped the windshield with a contraption he called a *Dingsda*, which my father also had a word for, I told him: thingamajig! He begged me to repeat it till he got the hang of it. We slid along the icy streets to the Uhlandstraße, originally named the Bismarckstraße, until someone complained that old man Otto wasn't really a Swabian!

As soon as we got cozy in the kitchen where we'd always spend the most time, Sybille ladled out a steaming bowl of what she called a bouillon concoction, with a raw egg cracked in at the last moment and garnished with homegrown parsley, courtesy of Capt. Cardunier's wife, Sybille noted. I recalled he commanded the French troops charged with, the charter read, "Securing and Protecting the Citizens of the French Zone," one of four Germany had been divided into. The captain took a special liking to Richard when he learned Richard had not only saved his Jewish wife but also did his best to sabotage German military vehicles he'd been obliged to repair in his garage and machine shop.

Slurping the broth down, we made a stab at catching up till Waldi yawned. So we all did and called it a night, because we'd be rising early to "harvest," Richard grinned, "the best little Christmas tree" I'd ever see.

On the way to the woods I confessed we'd never had a tree, not even a Hanukah bush, so that I'd have to make the rounds of Christian pals to get my fill of that "ur-odor."

Richard laughed, "Sybille not only demands a tree, she loves to boom out all the carols. In fact, she almost left her hiding place at the farm to steal a look at the miserable little excuse of one I propped up in the kitchen where she most liked to be. She so wanted to be there the moment Frau Braunfel lit the candles when I dropped by for what I always worried might not just seem likely a friendly visit, and we had to restrain Sybille from climbing down from the loft. The Germans made a habit of raiding possible hiding places especially during holidays, those cunning buggers. One major I had to report to about my repair work on their killing machines even announced with some glee, 'Jews love our Christmas trees!' He never suspected me, and even whispered some things the S.S. would have been 'gleeful' to learn about him. Given the right opportunity, I wouldn't have hesitated betraying his confidence, of course."

As we started down the lane toward some back woods overhung with fresh snow, a hedgehog trundled across our path. Richard had to slam on the brakes, throwing his arm across my chest as he did. "Once an uncle, teaching me to drive, almost beat me when I tried to avoid a squirrel and nearly rolled his car into a ditch," he barked. "Uncle Helmut put his hands around my neck and yelled, 'Whose life is more important, anyway, you numbskull!'" Of course, I was tremendously curious about Richard's work for the German military, not to say Nazis, but I never found the courage to ask questions beyond where he stopped.

I recalled that the Nazis stationed around Tuttlingen depended on him to keep their vehicles running, especially in winter, and other equipment functioning as well; that the tire gauge he'd invented was more accurate than other makes; and thus had questions about how he could continue "serving" them, seemingly aiding their effort. At the same time, it was clear he'd have done anything to protect Sybille, even with his own life. At any rate, he was never in much of a mood to say more than he did, which I was learning to respect more and more.

Caught up in such thoughts, I didn't realize Richard had stopped the car and was pointing to a spruce at the edge of the lane. "Let's have a look at that one. I'll get the axe from the trunk in case it passes inspection." He was already circling the tree while I fussed with my boots, finally able to push my door open against a snowbank.

"Can we just cut down any old tree around here?" I asked

him.

"Well, you can always report me to the officials, but that'd be the French occupation forces. They have total jurisdiction over all these outlying woods ever since they cleaned out the last pockets of German resistance. Right past where you're standing, over there." I followed his finger to a hollow cupped by an overhanging ledge. "What's left of a pillbox the French overran is still up there, if you want to trudge up for a look. You won't trip over any bodies, though you might stumble across some bones. A few town kids came across a skull a while back, and lit it up with a candle inside like a pumpkin. That jolted the local rag we have for a paper, and letters to the editor flew back and forth. My own little crude joke is that any flesh on those *Wildschwein* was devoured by the resident *jabalinas*."

"Thanks for the history lesson, Richard. That'll do nicely for now!" Which I regretted saying as soon as I said it. He looked away with some pain on his face.

Striding up to the tree he'd decided on, he took out a tape measure, having learned long ago just how big a tree he could handle by himself; not to mention just fit in under the ceiling. Sybille always insisted on the tallest he could manage. "Stupidly, I used to cut a tree down only to realize I couldn't lift the damn thing! They don't make glue strong enough to stick it back on its stump, so now I reach back to early trig memories, do some fancy figuring, check angles, and add a good dash of hunch. With you along to carry the heavy end," he winked, "I can be a little off, right? Of course, the real labor, make that nightmare, is getting it straight enough to satisfy you-know-who. And I don't mean Waldi, whose main job is to lap water from the stand so it doesn't flood the rug. I swear it's the closest we've come to divorcing. So now I think I'll just commission you chief proper-upper; and for once enjoy the negotiations!"

Richard just shook his head but kept his tongue when Sybille let me off easy vis-à-vis my pitiful efforts to align the tree so that it not only stood more or less straight, but also showed off its best side. When I said our fire department wouldn't approve of live candles, they said Tuttlingen's could use a little fire to practice on. The moment the sun went down and the dark deepened, Richard lit the candles while we belted out O Tannenbaum, first in German, then again in English by special request. With that devilish look, Richard brought out some pre-war schnapps his father had made, promising I'd remember its bite forever. "Don't know about that," I said in the morning, "because I can't remember a single thing post chugalugging our way down the whole bottle!"

"Not the worst of it," Richard grinned, "we couldn't stop you singing every carol you know. So loudly, so off-key, Waldi covered his ears with his paws."

To everyone's relief, the rest of the visit we did very little socially. Sybille even excused us from going round with her to deliver her holiday stollens. However, we did attend a gathering at Capt. Cardunier's quarters. He'd have understood, Sybille counseled, if we'd declined the invitation, but his wife would have taken offense. After we mingled for a while, some officers broke off into a corner. Richard whispered they'd be rehashing efforts to track down former Nazis, who were apparently still meeting in underground "cells" to stir up trouble of one sort or another. The soldiers grew louder the more they drank, so by and by we were all privy to their exchanges.

While there was laughter over some of the escapades they dissected, no one laughed when one drunk lieutenant said quite loudly that they do what the Nazis perfected—"take hostages and kill one every hour until the swastika-worshippers give themselves up!"

Richard put an end to the discussion, reminding everyone

he couldn't imagine any Nazi ever recriminating himself—especially not to save a fellow German. "I've heard them denounce their own, including me by the way, for not being brave enough to follow Adolf to the end of the thousand-year Reich, whatever the consequences," he said before apologizing to the ladies for mentioning such things at such a time. Then he asked me to drive Sybille home so he could spend a little more time with Capt. Cardunier, who was being called back to France for consultations.

While I had a valid Wisconsin license, I wasn't sure if it covered out-of-country travel. More to the point, I was scared about the prospect of anything happening to Herta, the Daimler named after Richard's mother, not to mention Sybille. "First," Richard said pulling his arm tight around my neck, "I think Sybille likes to be mentioned ahead of any automobile, even Herta. Second, if anything happens, Kramer's garage is always open for repairs. Third, as you know we're in with the French, so you could drive without a license altogether." He bowed to Sybille, who looked almost as concerned as I.

Herta kept making nasty grinding sounds, perhaps because I drove too slowly, not to mention in the wrong gear. One quick lesson wasn't enough for my rattled brain. It didn't help seeing Sybille in the rearview mirror keep her eyes closed the whole time, but somehow I got us back home without incident. Richard said not to worry, Herta needed a tune-up anyway. Whatever I did to her in that short distance wouldn't be all that costly. Then, because I was thinking of investing in a jalopy in the States, and business was slow over the holidays, Richard invited me along to watch Hermann, his chief mechanic, and him go over Herta.

"Treat this like a serious subject at school," Hermann said, handing me some overalls, "and you'll always know how to repair your own shit, because the boss is a master mechanic, knows cars like I know schnapps, which is to say from top to bottom and back." After Richard and he finished checking everything, replacing this and that, I said I should have taken notes.

Taking a sheaf of papers from his desk, Richard showed me the makings of a manual. "For idiots," he said sternly. "And before Hermann poisons me so he can take over the garage, I'd like to see it in print." He tossed a rag to Hermann, who yawned as if he'd heard that one before. "Going out for a smoke," Richard said. "See you don't do something really dumb in the meantime, boys!" We understood he also meant clean up the mess of the overhaul.

"If I don't get down and dirty, do all the underneath shit, which the arthritic spurs up and down the boss's crooked spine won't let him manage anymore, he'd lose even more business," Hermann whispered. When Richard returned, Hermann rambled on, and I wondered if he'd more nips from his "vitamin supplement" when he said, "How a smart Jew like Sybille stays married to a dumb goy is beyond human understanding. My slightly less bright wife, not a Jew, sorry to say, would match up better with you, Boss, want to trade?" Hermann's tone was so ominous I must have looked shocked, which brought on a bit of a truce between them, although Richard got off one last shot.

"You only get a Christmas bonus if your poor wife doesn't ring me up to pull you out of a snow bank one more time. Piss in the snow all you want. Hell, howl at the moon about how unfair life is, for all I care. But you better keep track of how much goes down your gullet so you make it back home before she gets up, got that?"

"Yes, sir!" Hermann clicked his heels, saluting limply. "Heil Kramer!" Then he bowed almost far enough to topple over before tiptoeing toward the heavy steel door, huffing and puffing his way out.

Richard tried explaining Hermann's "Jewish-thing," as he

called it, on the way back to Sybille's vintage supper. But neither of us could quite fathom what really lay behind Hermann's occasional outbursts. Richard's guess seemed as good as any: "Hermann's sitting on something, all right. If drink doesn't do him in, he might just erupt one of these days so we'll know from the fallout what's in his heart." I couldn't help thinking Richard was also sitting on something—that for all his good nature and principles might also have a dark understory.

Over her lovingly prepared dumplings and sauerkraut, Sybille and Richard argued lightly about when to exchange gifts. Richard had drifted away from early religious roots, as he put it, and he couldn't recall when or even with what ceremony childhood gifts had been exchanged. At least we'd agreed by mail several weeks back that each of us would only give the others one gift apiece, including Waldi, of course, who seemed to sense he'd better quit begging so much at supper. When I finally suggested we do gifts the night before I'd leave, on January 3, Richard licked his chops, went to the big calendar on the kitchen wall, drew a large circle around the third, and rubbed his hands.

On Christmas day, fighting off sleep after a heavy dose of roast goose and way too much dessert, we were sitting around pretending to read—Richard slightly miffed I wouldn't play any games, or even take him up on his offer to reveal some gaming secrets—when the phone rang. Sybille quickly handed it to me, her eyes widening. "It's from Milwaukee!" Stumbling toward her outstretched hand, Waldi on my heels, I sensed something was wrong, as my parents had written they'd be away visiting Chicago cousins, and likely try to call after New Year's.

"Rufus was hit by a car," my mother said so faintly I asked her to repeat, but she put my father on the phone. All I could think was why had Waldi begun to whimper, brushing up against my leg.

"Mother said Rufus is dead. We don't know how it could have happened. We'd left him with neighbors, who said they'd not let him roam for the short time we were away, because as you know, anyone but you out with him on a walk, he'd tear loose and pretend to be a wild wolf." Trailing off, Dad's voice mumbled something about burying him out back in the woods he loved, near several other childhood pets whose graves I'd mark with a little cross made of popsicle sticks I'd whitewash feverishly till Dad pulled me away.

"So the burying beetles can free his soul," I stammered. Ever since I learned about them, they were my first thought when anything died, human or animal. "Please don't replace him right away," I begged through tears. We'd always go out the very next day to replace dogs that died, which habit Gramma Anna set in motion early on. "Okay, cry today but tomorrow we get a new one!" she'd command.

Forgetting to say goodbye, I just limply handed the phone back to Sybille, who led the way to the sunroom, where Richard wouldn't be disturbed by our voices.

"So, pretend I'm your mother," Sybille began. "Assuming a normal mother-son relationship, you probably know you can tell her, well, me in this case, some things that may be harder to tell your father. Is that fair to suppose?" It was all the invitation I needed, so I hugged her till Waldi suddenly came at me, barking furiously.

"Shh, he's not a Nazi, you dodo!" Sybille pointed to his bed in the corner, and we waited till he finally lay down.

"Oh, Sybille, I've kept you up way too long, sorry!" I said after emptying a bucket of Rufus-tales. I'd missed him as much as anyone in the family, I confessed, which was why Waldi's company meant so much. Then I cleared the tea service while Sybille padded off to bed with a little wave.

Sybille was sharing the phone call in some detail with Richard when I entered the kitchen for breakfast. I asked for the day off, and Sybille said she'd pack a lunch to die for. "Into the woods with you, and here's a little map to find the baby Danube trickling along Tuttlingen's edge. You can be alone with your thoughts about Rufus there. If you like, Waldi would probably like to tag along," she added, at which point he jumped up, running off for his leash.

"I sometimes do my best listening, I should say recording, because I go on automatic when I'm about to nod off," Sybille said to me, "so none of what you were saying at that late hour was in vain, you see. And Richard has something 'funny' to add, by the way."

"Well," he began, "I had such a fascination for burying beetles as a youngster that my parents were worried I'd not have what they most wished for me, a normal childhood. The other kids would throw stones at my window to come play soccer, but I was often lost in my little collection of that elegant creature, without which, by the way, it's estimated we might not be here, or likely drown in detritus. They were like a little family to me, so I feel for you. I love knowing they recycle flesh that would soon stink up the place far more without their services. Did you know they're guided to corpses by a super-keen sense of smell? It sets them apart from all other beetles, which get by on touch with their feelers. Hey, my memory for certain things isn't shot, now is it!?"

"Wow, Richard, thanks for all that. It's good to have burying beetles in mind just now," I managed to say.

"At any rate, soon as I get back I have some gift wrapping to do for some souls around here," I said straight at Waldi, who bounced up on his hind legs the way Rufus used to. We were all relieved to put more talk of Rufus off and get ready for a night of gift-giving.

"So, better get back in time," Sybille cautioned, "and if you get lost in the woods Waldi will expect a tip for leading you back home."

After we pushed back from what Richard called our "penultimate supper"—he'd offered a toast to our "last supper" come spring, when they hoped I'd visit one more time before returning to the States—Sybille suggested we dress for the occasion, come up with costumes if the mood struck. She repaired to her room, Waldi under her arm; while Richard headed for the garage where he confessed he'd hidden his gifts, and I went off to my room to get ready for our midnight rendezvous at the foot of the tree.

Waldi's raucous barking as he shot out of Sybille's room was the opening fanfare. She had tied all manner of ribbons on him and capped his head with a hairnet, which he desperately tried shaking off. Below, in the garage, Richard boomed out "We Three Kings of Orient Are," which Sybille and I promptly turned into a round as we made our way majestically toward the tree. At first, we all looked straight ahead to honor the solemnity of the procession and avoid breaking up over our own costumes till we finished all the carol's verses, which Sybille knew by heart but Richard and I faked.

When I finally stepped back to take them both in, I nearly keeled over: they had studied photos of my parents I'd sent, effecting such close facsimiles I was rattled—Richard must have quickly cut his hair and shaped his mustache to match my father's, while Sybille sported a wig that mimicked my mother's way of wearing her hair. They weren't really close to my parents in size, so Sybille had put her sewing machine to work on clothes my parents, in cahoots, had sent some time ago. As loudly as possible, I hollered, "No damn fair, I've been had!" And they collapsed in laughter. Snarling, arching his back, even Waldi didn't recognize them.

"But Mother," Richard said to Sybille, looking me over, "who is this imposter?"

"I just hope our son's safe and sound in Tuttlingen, Father," Sybille warbled.

My simple-minded last-minute get-up got their heads shaking. I was trying for the look of the wild boar Richard had shot on a hunt he'd taken me on last fall, using one of Waldi's bones to fashion the fangs I clenched between my teeth. Admiring how they flared out of the corners of my mouth, Richard said he had some strong glue to fix the fangs permanently in my jaw.

"Okay, now we drink a little toast before gifting one another a little less frighteningly," Richard said, and made for the liquor cabinet to pour us a jigger of apricot brandy from his private reserve. "*Zum Wohl!*" he hooted and we lifted our jiggers on high. "That's one saying the Nazis couldn't corrupt."

"Rhymes with *skoal*," I chimed in. Downing our drinks, we clinked jiggers so hard they almost cracked.

"Now stomp on them and unite traditions," Sybille whooped.

On the train back to Darmstadt I took out the little game Richard had invented and carved by hand for me, complete with bitty figures to move about the miniature board. He'd attached a scroll of rules, followed by P.S.: "When totally frustrated, in possession of a fat headache for trying to beat yourself, not to mention heavy memories of buried things, I may let you in on my secret shortcut some fine day."

Knowing of my interest in acting, and that I was about to play Pyramus in the spring Shakespeare back at school in Darmstadt, Sybille gifted a lovely little edition of Shakespeare's plays in the famous SchlegelTieck translations, which she'd managed to save from her father's library before the Nazis ransacked it. "Here's to acting whatever role you're assigned with all your heart and soul," she'd written inside. I started a long letter of thanks I knew I couldn't finish.

Last Words

When the spring break of my last semester at the *Technische Hochschule* came round, I went off to the American Forces Club in town for one last, hot shower. The *TH*'s water ran "colder than a witch's tit," my roommates groused. Wanting to thank the staff for letting me enjoy an American breakfast now and then, I also hoped I'd run into Ken Sliman, the liaison officer at the American Consulate who'd supervised my year-long fellowship. However, he wasn't around, the desk clerk said. He'd been reassigned stateside and no one knew where to reach him. There were rumors his marriage was on the rocks, which I hoped wasn't true. Coincidentally, the clerk mentioned someone was on the way to the *TH* with my new passport, and he'd leave it with the administration. Recently out cycling, I'd fallen going too fast down a steep incline. It must have shot out of my rucksack, but I gave it up for lost after crawling around through the gorse. So this was beautiful news, because I wasn't certain my application for a new passport would clear in time to catch the Queen Mary out of Cherbourg, as planned, for the journey home.

If it hadn't come through when it did, it'd have been a real headache rebooking and all; but in the back of my mind I thought in that event I'd try to contact the Kramers one last time. I knew I should anyway, to make amends for my shabby behavior of late, even though I deserved to be written off. They'd wanted me back for the spring break, but I begged off with fake reasons, because I wanted to pursue my relationship with Miriam Pfungsheim.

Back at the *TH*, when I'd finished packing, Director Meyers and family invited me to their quarters for something "special" to drink by way of farewell, the note read, and to pick up my passport as well. Leading me into his study, the director said, "Do you approve of our new bartender?"

It was Professor Breiter! He was wearing smart white gloves, saluted and bowed. I rushed over to him with joy, while the Meyers family stood by, smiling broadly.

"Our specialty for such occasions," the director said, eyeing his new butler, "is tea laced with cognac. Sound all right to you?"

"Never had it, sir, but I'm sure game. Besides," I said, "I've come to value your medical facilities. If anything happens, I know I'll be nursed back to health!" On that note, Professor Breiter started pouring, and we started drinking, talking and laughing. Even Meyers' children were allowed a finger of cognac, just in case they'd develop a toothache from all the sweets on board, Mrs. Meyers said with a lilt. Right before I turned one last time to say thanks for the memories, little Peter, whom I'd become especially fond of, ran to the sideboard to fetch my passport, which we'd totally forgotten about. He'd wrapped it himself in expensive paper he'd decorated with little mice on a red, white, and blue background, because we shared a fondness for mice, a sizeable minority population at the *TH*, majoring in leftovers.

On my way out, I promised to send Peter an Indian headdress, then helped him slide down the hallway banister one last time. He sat down on the bottom step, waving the little wave of children, while Professor Breiter called down after me that he'd drive me all the way to Frankfurt in the morning to catch the express to Paris, thence to board the boat train to Cherbourg.

Deciding to stroll around the *TH's* grounds one last time, I found myself eventually in the little cemetery adjacent, staring down at the graves of Eva Breiter and the two Breiter children. I knelt to pick a few stray weeds when I heard a car approach on the access road beside the gravel walkway. Its lights were off so at first I couldn't make out who was at the wheel. When the professor himself stepped out, in his signature fedora, waving, I scrambled to my feet, about to apologize for intruding.

"My family's going to miss you and so shall I," he said, putting his arm around my shoulder and turning me to face their headstones. "I've caught sight of you here before." I was still holding the weeds I'd picked, which he gently relieved me of. "Here, let me have those. I should be taking better care of their resting places. The Nibelungs, you know, had it right—one must keep consecrating hallowed ground where loved ones lie. Your President Lincoln also had some words on the subject, as I recall." We stood for a while, not saying anything, listening to the music of insects in the trees. "I'd offer you a ride to the house," Professor Breiter said, finally, "but I can imagine you'd rather take the slow road back by yourself on your last night, correct?" I nodded and he left, calling out the car window, "I'll be sure to get you up in time if that stupid alarm in your room doesn't go off. It's a Big Ben, after all. No wonder our Swiss industrialist co-conspirators can make clocks and guns at the same time. That work, alas." I sensed he just wanted to hang that in the air, so I didn't say anything in return.

He had breakfast on the table when I came down to the kitchen. "Americans like pancakes, I believe, so I've made you a stack from my grandmother's old recipe. Stuffed with cinnamon apples. As a young girl, she was taken to Paris and treated to a fancy spread of crêpes suzette, which made such an impression she begged the chef for the recipe. He'd come out himself in his magnificent hat and a huge starched apron, she recalled, and wrote it right out for her then and there on 'a real cloth napkin,' she'd say ever after. And he signed it with a flourish, 'like a great artist,' she'd end on with a big smile. He did tell her mother, my great grandmother, to withhold the cognac till grandmother's eighteenth birthday, which became a family mantra of sorts.

I'm sorry to say you're only getting a bastardized version—no hot orange-butter sauce, but there is a splash of cognac in there somewhere, because I dare say you're way past eighteen by now."

Tearing into the tasty cakes, I held back telling him I'd actually turned eighteen only the past July. He sat there sipping his coffee, watching me eat my fill. "My children used to eat just like that," he laughed, "unable to chew one mouthful without stuffing in more! My wife tried making a rule, they couldn't talk till they swallowed, but we soon gave up ... God, if only I'd died with them." Mumbling something about seeing to the car in the garage to make sure it would start, he motioned for me to leave everything when I finished. After dropping me off at the station in Frankfurt, he planned to visit a friend who oversaw the *Goethe Haus*. I recalled Miriam once suggesting we go see where old man Goethe carried on with all those women.

It was still early, so while the professor offered to load my suitcase and duffel bag into the trunk, I signaled I'd take in the trees out back, where we'd sometimes sit and talk about life. He pointed to the darkening sky, threatening a storm. "Don't take too long, the road can turn slippery in a downpour. Where's Goethe when we need him, anyway?" he said. "More light!" He knew I knew those were Goethe's last words.

We students had once sat around with the professor for a beer after class. Uncharacteristically jolly and relaxed, he steered the conversation toward famous "last words," which he mostly supplied, as none of us had made a habit of collecting any yet. "My favorite's Kafka's," he had said. "I pray I'll be up to something remotely as witty and, well, perfectly in character when my time comes. Now, this may be quite apocryphal, but Kafka is said to have said when his physician refused to administer more morphine—remember, he was in terrible pain, wracked by TB—'Kill me or you're a murderer!'" Professor Breiter waited for our reaction, but no one had as yet heard of Kafka, much less read him. Breiter promised, if he lived long enough, he'd teach a semester-long seminar on Kafka even if he had to kill to see it approved by the damnable curriculum committee. And besides, he'd also see Kafka crowned as the century's most prophetic writer.

We drove along in silence out to the autobahn to Frankfurt, though the professor cursed at a sleek Mercedes hurtling by, nearly blowing us off the road. In a stretch without much traffic, he hummed snatches of tunes I didn't recognize. Leaving the last of the Merck-Complex buildings well behind, he said something about their being storehouses for "whoring and healing." It was clear I wasn't expected to add anything. Finally, we pulled into the holding area outside the Frankfurt station, well ahead of my train's departure. Removing his well-worn driving gloves, Professor Breiter took out a pipe I'd never seen him smoke, tamped in some dark, pungent tobacco and struck a match, only to let it go out again.

Suddenly turning grave, he said, "I'm going to leave you with a serious injunction. I realize you came to us all fired up to continue with your math and science pursuits. And my colleagues on their side of the divide tell me you're not without talent, have some real promise and all—poor old Klarner couldn't get over your solving some equation or other, which had even baffled him for some time." I didn't open my mouth to say I had no idea what he was referring to. "But when it's time to consider graduate studies," he went on forcefully, "I think you ought to seriously consider going on in German." He paused to light another match, but it went out as well when he continued.

"If I had a few more years to pound things into your sometimes stubborn noggin, I think you could actually consider devoting yourself full-time to writing in German, like a few other souls whose mother tongue also wasn't German." He paused to roll down the window to clear the windshield of mist from our breath. "All this, of course, is no guarantee you'll reach the sort of maturity we expect from a real writer. In other words, my friend, it'll be a long journey."

As I sat there dumbfounded, he hopped out, popped the trunk open, and hoicked my bags out without a mention of staying in touch. But I think he knew I'd write. He did remove his fedora, waving it like a cowboy when I looked back through the station doors.

I knew I was supposed to feel some sort of thrill it was the Queen Mary's last voyage I'd booked without even knowing it. Most everyone was bursting with excitement, signing up left and right for the daily tours ranging all over the Queen's byways, many of which we were told had never been open to the public before. Everything was also highlighted, from the commemorative salt- and pepper-shakers to the embossed pillowcases. Not knowing a soul, I didn't have to refuse invitations flying back and forth between passengers who'd otherwise have never struck up a conversation at a bus stop on a snowy day. I did make my way to the railing for a bit of fresh air from time to time, but missed the passing of a whale and sighting of the Queen Elizabeth in mid-ocean on her way back to Europe—which had been announced as an event not to be missed. My ears almost came off, however, when the ships blasted their whistles at each other.

I did manage to save the farewell menu, because a painting of the ship, reproduced in full colors for the cover, said "save me or you'll regret it." Mostly, however, I buried myself in my bunk, nodding to third-class cabin-mates as they came and went, while I pored over every note I'd taken in my *TH* courses, reconstructing the whole year before it tumbled down the well of forgetting. Exhausted, I had to be jostled awake when we landed. Cabin-mates shook their heads when I didn't rush topside to wave back at the Statue of Liberty.

Clearing customs readily, I made my way through the throng to catch a cab to the airport for the flight back to Milwaukee. I had absolutely no desire to take in the sights of New York, though urged by everyone back home to do so, even postpone returning, since Wisconsin State's fall term wouldn't be starting soon.

My parents could have accused me of withdrawing, because I sequestered myself in the new bedroom they'd added on for me. Mom had convinced Dad I'd need to spend my last year at home in relative peace and quiet, given the active lives my younger sister and brother were starting to lead. I showed up for meals and was still chief dishwasher, but otherwise I spent most waking hours trying to figure out what I'd been up to, exactly, and where I might next be headed.

Professor Breiter's "injunction" heavily in mind, I made certain I had enough credits to complete math and science majors so I could enroll in as many German courses as possible before graduating, to see where they might take me. To put it mildly, I did less than distinguished work in most of my courses. I told myself it was due to spending so much time on panels upon returning; "to promote international understanding, especially among young people," advertising flyers insisted. My exchange year having been widely reported in Milwaukee papers, invitations mounted. Somehow managing to earn a respectable grade point average by the time it came to apply for graduate work at the state university, I still faced the nagging question of what course or courses to pursue, inasmuch as I was still totally undecided.

It never occurred to me to seek counseling, but when Professor Breiter learned I was still hedging and sent an exasperated letter urging me to talk "to someone with an overview of my options," I came to my senses. A fellow student happened to mention really profiting from a session with the director of career counseling, so I finally made an appointment, which my mother asked to be in on. She seemed more and more worried I might be losing my way.

In an initial meeting, the director reviewed my record and advised that I take home aptitude and assorted other tests. When I returned them along with some quotes from Professor Breiter's letters, she seemed eager to hear what he had to say about my prospects from his vantage point. "I'll need another week to digest everything here," she said. "The secretary will schedule another meeting for your mother and you."

By the time we arrived, Mom and I both had a case of nerves. Mine, because decision time was finally at hand; but hers, she suddenly confessed, because of the possibility I'd continue with German studies at a much more serious level. "I keep talking to Gramma about things," she said softly, "and hope she's not turning in her grave." Startled, I asked what that was all about. She said she'd tell me later, after I did the dishes and we could pair off to the den.

Waving us into her suite, the director of counseling let us get comfortable before starting in. "Whatever you decide, please take what I'm going to say as just another opinion. Informed, I hope, but I really can't ever be sure," she began. Mom shifted in her chair. I looked over at her hard, because I knew she'd hide her own feelings, sometimes doing so from herself as well; and she never gave advice, just listened.

"Colleagues who know of Professor Breiter's work, his reputation, have persuaded me to take what he says very seriously," the director said at first, to my astonishment. "That said, I can be quite brief it turns out. Even if you do continue work in German, the best science schools, medical schools as well, still require some grounding in foreign languages, especially Latin and German. So you'd be protected, so to speak, by forging ahead with German, if only for a while."

I did have vague thoughts of doctoring I might have conveyed to Gramma at some point, though she would tell anyone I'd make the perfect judge to try the "evil devils" who brought so much misery to the world, not to mention our own flesh and blood, even as she waved off questions about what had really happened to her family after the Germans retreated from their botched Russian campaign. Suddenly awash in that memory, I had to concentrate harder when the director continued.

"Let me add a complication because of some things in your record, as well as the report we received from Director Meyers about your efforts at the *TH*." Removing her reading glasses, she looked me straight in the eye. "You can also use your considerable German to pursue a career in the Foreign Service. Do you know they're looking for qualified officers at this time to help ferret out former Nazis, not to mention stabilize the new, democratic German government? Some contacts we enjoy say our military are having a hard time finding out who did what in the war years." Excusing herself for a moment, she let that sink in. Mom looked quizzically over at me, but I could only shrug my shoulders. No one had ever raised that possibility. I searched my memory—had Mr. Sliman perhaps mentioned anything of that sort, given what his office did? Not that I could recall. My brain began shutting down—too many flavors—just give me vanilla, I kept thinking.

"Well," the director said when she returned, "that's a lot to ponder, I realize. But you don't have to decide anything just yet. So why not go ahead, apply for a place in German, as well, say, in math, and, what, even chemistry too, was it? And for good measure, why not take the Foreign Service exam when you get to Madison, and let what happens shape your next moves? In any event, it won't really hurt you in the long run to postpone more consequential decisions for a while."

"Talk about playing into your hands," Mom said when we left. "Mr. Procrastinator Extraordinare!" I wondered if most mothers knew their sons as well as she knew me …

"Okay, I'll get Dad off your back," she said when we got home. "You have enough to worry about. Of course we'd appreciate being let in on any decisions, if you can decide anything at all!" I kissed her smack on the spot on her cheek she pointed to, locked myself in my room after hanging a sign on the door to keep my sister and brother at bay, put Mozart's Third Violin Concerto on the phonograph, which Gramma had gotten me listening to years back, and didn't know what in hell I'd do till I did it.

Stories

Beautiful, Innocent Music

O<small>N</small> Monday, November 11, everyone woke up to the news that the Germans, given seventy-two hours to accept armistice terms, finally agreed, and a day began we still celebrate. Eddie had the urge to lean on the Pevner kid, still delivering papers shouting NO MORE WAR! up and down Eddie's block. "Lend me a bundle and I'll make us both a bundle pitching them in the Polish neighborhoods you better avoid. Remember that bloody nose Schnooty Palcz sent you home with, right?" Eddie yelled from his stoop, but the kid beat it around the corner.

"Come and get your Humpty Dumpty eggs!" Eddie's mother yelled from the kitchen. "There'll be plenty of time later to drink as many orange sodas as you want, while your father, Uncle Max and I drink the dandelion wine you helped me make last summer." Max eventually tootled by mid-morning, parking his horse and dairy wagon in the alley. He'd already had so much to drink in such a short time he couldn't have roughed Eddie up even if he'd wanted to.

Milwaukee's civic leaders hastily arranged a series of city-wide celebrations, first in the separate ethnic neighborhoods, even the German blocks, then building to an endless parade down Wisconsin Avenue till the grand finale, complete with fireworks. So much confetti and other objects flew out of upper windows along the route that volunteers were called for to help with the clean-up so the city's coffers wouldn't take a nasty hit.

As far as Eddie's father was concerned, the best news was that not only was Emil Sauer's previously announced concert not cancelled, but he would offer several more free concerts as well "in honor of our glorious victory," the note in the newspaper read, and all tickets already purchased would be refunded! Even Max thought he might tag along, though he got to thinking of his lost son and said, "Couldn't hardly sit there without him at my side. I'd just muck the whole night up with my misery."

Eddie's mother patted Max's cheek and stuffed another chunk of bacon into his mouth. "You may be my sister's boy, Maxie, but you break my heart sometimes, too."

"Beautiful, innocent music," Eddie's father said on the way to the Pabst Theater for Emil Sauer's concert, and whistled a few melodies to set the stage for what he promised would be a concert to remember till the end of time. But just before the streetcar stopped he blurted out, "Good God, I almost forgot! You go ahead, I'll catch up." He handed Mrs. Hahn the tickets for Eddie and her and walked briskly back toward their house. When they were settling into their seats, the houselights dimming, Mr. Hahn slipped through the side curtain, sat down at the end of their row, and propped a huge doll on his lap, to everyone's astonishment. "You two aren't the only ones capable of working on a secret project," he whispered, then softly introduced them to Emil Sauer, Jr., a large creature he'd been busy manufacturing out of leftovers from his tailoring trade over many months.

The very next minute the maestro walked out on the stage and took a bow before he sat down at the piano, nonchalantly flipping his tux's tails back over the bench before dialing it up a notch, while Mr. Hahn bounced the doll on his knee and waved its arm.

Mrs. Hahn suffered her usual embarrassment whenever Mr. Hahn did strange things in public, but this was almost more than her nerves could bear. She tried to push back into the shadows as people started turning their way, because Mr. Hahn's manipulations of Emil Sauer, Jr. were not exactly noiseless.

The maestro, quite nearsighted, could barely see past the first few rows, so all he sensed was that there was some fuss to the rear, but he was determined to quiet the house and plunged into the first piece, a Chopin mazurka. Tapping time while following the music with his eyes closed, Mr. Hahn turned the doll over and over on his lap. When the last chords evaporated and the audience started clapping, he worked the doll's hands into something of a thudding clap he continued producing after the applause died down.

By intermission, Mrs. Hahn had managed to rein in his enthusiasm some, even getting Mr. Hahn to lay the doll on the floor. "Please give him a much-needed rest, my love," she said in the voice she'd developed over many a similar incident. However, she was too embarrassed to leave her seat, fearful that they'd run into someone they knew, who'd be bound to inquire about the goings-on in their aisle. Careful to oblige her at this point and avoid a stretch of silence in their daily doings, Mr. Hahn took Eddie out to the lobby for a soda, but not before fussing with some threads on the doll's suit, which he'd even decked out with a vest, his specialty. He kept a file of orders of his vests from "certain people," he liked to tease, adding if he were immodestly inclined to drop a name, people would surely recognize a "certain general, as well as a certain admiral, not to mention Milwaukee's socialist mayor."

Just as Emil Sauer started in on a Chopin ballade to begin the second half of the concert, he seemed to suffer something like an asthma attack, clutched his chest, and turned sideways on the bench away from the audience, stretching his arms as far out as he could manage. One could hear him gasp, while stagehands ran to his side from the wings. At that very moment, Mr. Hahn stood up suddenly, ran up the aisle, and hurled Emil Sauer, Jr. onto the stage. The maestro stopped gasping for a moment, his eyes widening, and looked at the doll as if it were alive. Managing to get some strength back, he waved off the stagehands and lifted the doll up onto the piano bench, carefully positioning it so its puffy hands sat on the keys. Then he brushed himself off and, bowing deeply to the audience, left the stage under his own power. We later learned he'd kept walking till he reached the Milwaukee River, where he could catch enough deep breaths to clear his head. The papers reported he took the next train out of town, his trunks sent on after him.

 Mr. Hahn, meanwhile, had sat rooted in his seat long after the curtain had fallen and the theater was empty. Later he said all he could think was that the sight of the doll at the piano was "dastardly wrong," so he finally made his way to the stage, gathered Emil Sauer, Jr. up in his arms and cradled him home on the streetcar. Mrs. Hahn, who knew he'd need time to return to his senses, had already led Eddie back home. Nobody said a word when Mr. Hahn returned with the doll asleep on his shoulder. He trudged up to the attic and, covering it with an old blanket, laid it back in the coffin he'd ordered some time ago to be buried in himself. "What a strange state I was in," was all he said the next morning. Everyone seemed greatly relieved when the victory celebrations subsided and things more or less returned to normal.

The Class of 1922

When the lists were posted for which two students would walk side by side down the aisle together at North Division High's graduation exercises, Schnooty and Eddie, given the separation between their surnames, drew different partners. Schnooty could have lived with the arrangement if his partner were almost anyone except Bertha McNit, he said. Called "Big Bertha" by some of the nastier boys, she kept protesting all during the war years that she wasn't a German weapon and begged them not to torment her. Schnooty said he was afraid he'd jump out of line and bop the first guy who said "boom boom" when they walked past, which might have cost him his diploma. Eddie wasn't sure he wanted Schnooty to try to finagle their marching together, even for old time's sake, because Henrietta Hooper, with whom Eddie was paired, although aloof and not known for fooling around, ever, with any boy in the county, was something of a beauty. Eddie thought it would make quite a statement to "certain people" in the audience if he were at Henrietta's side. But as usual, Eddie finally gave in—Schnooty was probably going to hang around for life one way or another, and a stroll down the aisle together wasn't exactly a marriage proposition. Up to his usual cunning ways, in no time Schnooty managed to arrange a swap, while getting everyone involved to shut up about it so no teacher would bolix the maneuver at the last minute.

The Hahns, Eddie's parents, gave their extra tickets to Gertie Meister and her best friend, Ida Emmert, who were both juniors. Schnooty was trying to get serious with Ida, who toyed with him the way she did with any boy stupid enough to try to get her to go steady, which meant first of all he had to go through Gertie, because that's how they dealt with "the wolf pack," they both joked. Gertie knew that would always be her role around any really attractive girl she'd be drawn to, and relished talking tough if she had to, playing her part to the hilt.

When the incidental music headed into its last bars and the auditorium was bulging with bodies, Ida began biting her nails. Gertie had worked on her more than usual to help with a plan to do something wild during the ceremony so the boys would always remember the moment. The girls had practically skipped the last week of classes, but Ida kept waffling, scared there'd be serious consequences, until Gertie promised she'd do most of the dirty work.

"Come on, Ida," she finally said, with an edge Ida could never disobey. "All you have to do is carry the damn birdcage into the auditorium when I give the signal. Don't worry your little fuzzy head. It'll be all wrapped up so no one will have a clue. It'll look like we're bringing stuff for the festivities afterward. Counting on you, Ida Emmert! I promise you Schnooty will finally take some notice of you, kiddo. As for Eddie, let's just say he won't ever forget me. Besides, I love to make him squirm—brings out his adorable side."

Trying to get past the mention of the birdcage, Ida said, "I know I'm not as smart as you, Gertie Meister, but a birdcage?" Gertie ran a finger across Ida's lips, took her by the hand, and led her all the way down Burleigh Avenue to Pete's Pet Shop, where her cousin Freddy worked. They waited until he finished with a customer who was trying to decide between two puppies, then he took the girls behind the curtain to the stockroom.

"Meet Mryna the mynah," Freddy said. "Pete agrees you can rent her for seven bucks for one night, but I talked him down to a five spot. How's that for a loving act from a dear cuzz?" Gertie gave him one of those cut-the-shit looks. He looked offended but straightened his bow tie and bowed; at which so did Myrna, who on cue promptly rattled off the words that Gertie, with Freddy's help, had been teaching her for some time. Ida nearly fainted, partly from sheer delight, partly at the prospect of what would happen when Gertie unwrapped the cage and cued Myrna to perform just as the seniors were marching out to the strains of "Pomp and Circumstance." But Ida refused to go along unless Gertie promised Myrna would be kept under wraps until the last possible moment.

Awkwardly hefting the birdcage between them, Gertie and Ida timed their arrival so that Eddie's parents were already seated, as was most of the crowd. Luckily, their seats were on the aisle so they slid in just as the orchestra struck up. No one took notice when they wedged the cage in between their seats. Gertie heard Myrna rustling around under the towel and tapped a finger on the top knob, which quieted the bird, while Ida slunk lower in her seat, sticking her nose in the program.

Occasionally, while the ceremony droned on, the graduates in the front rows grew restless, and Myrna let loose a few sounds. "She's just warming up, all great singers do that," Gertie whispered when Ida looked like she'd bolt. At first, no one else seemed to notice except Eddie, who'd swiveled his head around a few times to grin their way.

"Whatcha got under there?" A man sitting across the aisle leaned over, saying it again for good measure, his voice fairly booming. The Hahns stiffened when all the graduates spun around, too, the very moment the class valedictorian was reaching the climax of her speech. She broke off mid-sentence, stared out over the footlights, and promptly lost her place.

Myrna must have sensed the tension, because she flapped her wings so hard she almost knocked the cage over. Gertie had no choice but to act then and there. Quickly unwinding the towel, she opened the door to the cage, raised it to clear the seat in front, tilted it so the bird found itself sliding out and began cawing, "Myrna want a cracker?"

As people ducked, covering their heads, even shrieking, Myrna flew straight toward the stage, circled the dignitaries a few times, and finally perched on the wire stretching across from both wings, flying a large banner in the school's colors: CONGRATULATIONS TO THE CLASS OF 1922! One of the newspaper's photos the next day showed a sea of faces upturned as one, while an opposite photo featured Myrna as a sort of crown over the dignitaries' heads. The lead article reported no one said a word or budged from their seats until long after Myrna cawed again as if to clear her throat, then rasped out, "Eddie and Schnooty, go team, rah rah rah!" At least that's what people in the front rows said they could distinctly hear, and Mr. Hahn claimed the bird stuck in "some mighty nice cuss words" for good measure.

As if waiting for an excuse to celebrate on its own terms, the class suddenly raised Eddie and Schnooty up on a dozen shoulders and headed for the football stadium. The principal, thinking his position might be in jeopardy, had all he could do to repair to his office, where one suspected he tried writing out versions of a letter of resignation; while the vice-principal, who was the boys' biggest cheerleader, had the good sense to hoick the box of diplomas onto his shoulder and follow the crowd. Eventually provided an escort by the football team, he was lustily cheered when, overcome with inspiration, he decided to throw the diplomas up over the crossbar of the goalpost and into their arms as the graduates ran by, shouting "hike" to cue each student.

After the field had cleared of the last stragglers, a clean-up crew arrived to haul away the trash — pitched programs, dozens of diploma ribbons, even discarded bits of clothing, and not a few bottles of homemade brews. Schnooty was still on his back in one end zone, Ida nestled beside him holding one hand tight, while his free arm stretched up at the night's new stars. "See that dark blue one, Ida?" He stuck out a finger. "That's Myrna up there! And I'm going to follow her as soon as I get my wings. Up, up, up and away!" Ida put her cheek to his. He kissed her lightly, fumbled with the ribbon from his diploma and, looping it around her neck, drew it into a neat little bow.

In the other end zone, Gertie was teasing Eddie mercilessly. She'd asked to see his diploma, but as soon as he handed it over she started running such fast circles around him he soon gave up trying to reclaim it and slumped to the turf. He didn't even try to snatch it when she poked it at him, so she finally just hit him on the head with it, dropping it in his lap. At that moment, something welled up in him. He stuck out an arm and pulled her down by the ankle. Before she could open her mouth, he pressed his lips so hard on hers her arms shot out from her sides; then she softly closed them around his neck till he came up for air.

"Well, I never ... Did you ever ..." That was the greeting all over town the next few weeks, as total strangers stopped to exchange sentiments about a graduation now most took for their own. Even Pete, the pet shop owner, got into the spirit, telling a much relieved Gertie—for her part she was determined to pay him back if Myrna didn't return—that he couldn't imagine better publicity. He installed both girls behind a little table to sign autographs one whole day; and Gertie drew a big fat mynah under her signature.

Oddly, only Mr. Hahn went another way with his emotions. Yes, he was happy no one was punished, not even the principal, not to mention the girls, who'd become overnight heroines. But when the Hahns invited Gertie, Ida, and Schnooty for a private celebration, he started in on a story he'd never recounted before. "Back in my student days in Budapest, I was an avid follower of

Louis Kossuth" — he didn't bother saying who that was, exactly — "and we were marching down the main boulevard with a banner right behind the great leader he was, spearheading a protest parade of workers and students, when the police suddenly charged us from all directions swinging their cudgels …" His voice gave out, so Mrs. Hahn motioned to start in on the borscht to give him a moment to recover from "that dark memory," is all he would say when he came back to himself, leading them in a blessing, half in Hungarian, before he lit the candles. For once, he didn't serve himself first, insisting that "our fine young souls here deserve first helpings," after which, for the remainder of the evening, he directed the conversation toward the rest of their lives, urging them to "march on with hearty hopes and dreams, hoisting their banners on high."

Babies in Boats

THOUGH it was only mid-afternoon when Eddie reached the Meisters' house, the shades were drawn. He noticed that the little porch hanging out over the driveway from an upstairs hallway was starting to come away from the siding, so he backed down into the street again to park at the curb. Paint was peeling under the front bay window he could see when he climbed the steps to the sweeping front porch. The big hickory swing he'd sometimes sat in, waiting for Gertie to get ready for their date, or afterward before they kissed goodnight, was hanging from a broken chain. Leaves and rolled-up newspapers lay scattered along one side. Thinking no one was home, perhaps even hadn't been for some time, he thought he'd better have a look all around, so he retreated without knocking and lit out toward the small, fenced-in back yard where the Meister's pet beagle normally lived in a goofy doghouse Gertie and he had slapped together and painted an ugly purple in one of Gertie's crazier moods.

The cellar windows seemed secure, but when he got to the milk chute near the back, the other side of which opened in the kitchen, its little door was stuck open. He could hear muffled sobs inside. He nearly pulled the chute's door off its hinges, and forced his face into the opening. Gertie was sitting at the table, head in hands, crying and crying. Mr. Meister, trying to comfort her, jumped up when Eddie called out. Still in his bathrobe, his torn undershirt hanging out, Felix Meister unlocked the door and limply shook Eddie's hand. Gertie stopped crying for a moment, looked over at Eddie, pushed a chair toward him, and started crying again. Eddie sat down quietly, waiting for them to speak first. Mr. Meister opened the ice box, and Eddie could see it was mostly bare except for a moldy grapefruit, a half-filled pitcher, and something in a casserole dish.

"All I can pour you is some iffy lemonade," Mr. Meister said, picking up the grapefruit and plunking it in the garbage pail. "This here, I'm afraid," he said pointing to the casserole, "is for my wife. Anna's dying of liver cancer, you know." He said it matter-of-factly, as if the whole world knew. "The doctor thinks as soon as she refuses another bite, then it won't be much longer. So far," he said with no emotion, "she's still taking a little macaroni and cheese." Lifting the cover of the dish, he sniffed it. "Here, Gittl," he said using his pet name for Gertie, "what do you think? Still good?"

Gertie wiped her eyes and put her nose to the dish. "It's okay, Pop. Good another day or two. Besides, Mama's not about to wolf it down the way she used to." Then, as if Eddie were a cook she needed to consult, she asked him, "Maybe I should have added Worcestershire sauce and some lemon rind? I just didn't think they'd be good on her queasy stomach, you know."

Eddie put his hand on top of hers, which felt lifeless; but he couldn't find any words. For a while they all sat there as if in a tableau. Finally, Eddie managed, "Would it, would it be at all possible to look in on your mother for a moment? I don't think I've ever told her what a perfect daughter she's raised." Gertie smiled a little through more tears, took his hand and led him to the steep stairs, while Mr. Meister said he needed a nap, now that a substitute nurse was on the job.

Her hand stuck to the newel, Gertie stopped at the first landing. She waited until Eddie came right up behind her, and said softly over her shoulder, "I sort of have a desire to marry you sooner rather than later, but I just can't act on it now, Ed. Can you live with that a while longer?"

He nuzzled up to her ear and whispered, "I've been on an

island somewhere, where nothing much has come true till now." Putting his hands to the small of her back, he gently pushed her up the rest of the way. For once they were perfectly balanced, though when Mrs. Meister's Angora cat, which had been watching them at the top of the stairs from between the balusters, came out of nowhere, taking a swipe at their feet, they tumbled over each other, hanging on to keep from falling back down the stairs.

"What is all that commotion, what is going on outside my door?" Anna Meister said when they peeked around the corner to see if she was sleeping. She held out her arms that used to be fat, cupping her hands behind their heads to draw them toward her, and both Gertie and Eddie kissed her on the cheek. "Welcome to my pink boudoir," she winked at Eddie. "Not many men can afford the admission," she managed to laugh a little. "So, young man, what brings you to my bedside, if I may put it somewhat indiscreetly." She was off and larking, a much younger version of herself.

"Well, I've always wanted to tell you," Eddie said, suddenly talkative, "that you not only grow beautiful roses, you've also raised a perfect daughter. I mean you and Mr. Meister have done something right," which he quickly felt he shouldn't have added.

"Gertie, watch out for this fellow. He'll say anything to get in your good graces," Mrs. Meister said, motioning them to sit on her bed a bit. Soon they were chatting about her garden and the roses she thought would win a prize in the neighborhood competition in the spring. "But as for Gertie's no-good father— now that I can't supervise him, he'll be sure to prune back my favorites way too much," she managed to get in before she lost energy, couldn't get another word out, so Gertie signaled Eddie it was time to go. When they turned around in the door for a last look, Mrs. Meister waved them back to whisper, "If you wait too long, I won't be in on any wedding plans, dearies." Her eyes closed and her cat, slithering between Gertie and Eddie, jumped up on the bed. Without opening an eye, Mrs. Meister reached out a finger to tickle its nose till it purred.

Up from a refreshing nap, Mr. Meister said he wanted to be alone with his Anna to say some things he couldn't or wouldn't if anyone else was around. He insisted Gertie and Eddie go out for a bite to eat. "Just bring me some nice leftovers, and if as I hope you go to Blini's Deli, and if they have strawberry-rhubarb pie, I need at least two pieces. Harry's still an easy mark, will let you flip him double or nothing," he said, giving them a two-headed coin. "In which case bring me the whole blooming pie!"

"Pop, Harry's onto this coin. How about the one with two tails? That, he might fall for with his poor eyesight," Gertie said, brightening up for the first time in some time. She went to find a scarf so she wouldn't have to fuss with her hair, and sent Eddie out to see what it might take to fix the swing if they could ever get around to fixing it. When she came out and saw what he was driving, she did a double-take. Eddie had pulled the rumble seat up to give her a good look at the coupe. When he offered to pop the hood as well, she politely declined, but said at some point she'd be curious to know just how he acquired such a sporty car — and anything else he had to confess. She said that dusting a mop of hair that had fallen over his eyes. When he didn't insist on knowing exactly what that gesture was supposed to mean, it was such restraint that made her think more than anything that they could last a lifetime together.

For his part, he knew that, given how long they'd parted to test the relationship, he'd eventually have to tell her where he felt he was heading next, especially about a tentative plan to take over Mr. Langjoen's drugstore, where he'd been working since getting his pharmacy papers. She knew he'd passed the final exam, albeit barely.

Soon Gertie and Eddie were slurping up chocolate phosphates

and gorging on Harry Blini's famous corned beef sandwiches, cured to perfection, he boasted, from an old secret family recipe. When they finished, Gertie wiped Eddie's mouth, then he wiped hers, before they spun around the usual three times on their stools for luck, their knees bumping. They were starting for the coat rack when they caught sight of a couple arguing at a little table under the front window. Gertie whispered not to stare, but Eddie couldn't take his eyes off them. First, the woman twirled her ring, then the man twisted his, then they stared out the window in opposite directions. The man turned back suddenly, catching Eddie staring. He held up his plate and said loudly, "I'm having the pecan pie, and my wife's having the mint chocolate cheesecake. What the damn else would you like to know?" His glare took in Gertie, too.

Gertie mumbled something about being sorry, and pulled Eddie, who'd frozen in embarrassment, up to the register. The little scene seemed to wipe away the couple's troubles for the moment, because the man fed his wife a piece of his pie, and she spooned some cheesecake onto his tongue. They weren't exactly smiling, but they didn't seem as anxious anymore

At the register, Harry Blini said he'd heard about Mrs. Meister's struggle and sent along a whole pie, with a little jar of dill pickles for Mr. Meister. "To snack on in the middle of a sleepless night," Harry said softly. He did insist on keeping the two-headed coin, which he planned to use in a necklace for his granddaughter. They all agreed it was a fitting climax to Felix Meister's career as a con artist.

Gertie made up a cot in the basement for Eddie to spend the night. About to say goodnight, he noticed an old table half in the dark near the coal bin. A net sagging in the middle stretched across. "Ping-Pong, anyone?" he said when he spotted a crock underneath stuffed with balls and paddles, most of which were covered with nicks and dents.

"You're on!" Rubbing her hands, Gertie spit into them. She hit the light switch, but only two of the overhead light bulbs came to life, one over each end of the table, while the two sockets over the middle had no bulbs at all, they soon noticed. "Be a good test of our night vision," she said serving up a wicked spin that blooped over the net, skidding onto the floor before Eddie could stretch out to backhand it.

"You're about to regret that," he said, slapping his paddle against his other hand till it hurt. "Ladies first, serve!"

Trading nasty smashes—her forehand was superior to his, but his backhand pretty much evened things out—they soon worked up a sweat and were about to swing into a pattern of nice long rallies when something came over Gertie—a twinge, perhaps, of what her mother was feeling upstairs on her deathbed, and Gertie put so much force into the next return Eddie had to duck. The ball shot up toward the ceiling. The next thing they knew the lights went out. Gertie told Eddie not to move. It was so dark anyone not familiar with the clutter would soon sport a bump on the noggin; she was going to get a flashlight. Grateful to obey because he favored the dark—they used to argue about turning out lights—he just stood there, slowing his breathing.

Gertie didn't return for some time, because she'd had to wake her father when she couldn't find a flashlight, or even some matches, as apparently all the house lights had gone out; and of course he had to tell her straight away how her mother was doing at the moment.

"I'm surprised you didn't crawl around till you found the cot," Gertie said when she caught Eddie in the flashlight's beam still standing there as if in a trance. She took his hand and walked him around looking for the fuse box. When they found the blown fuse and replaced it, nothing happened. It was too late to call an electrician. "Well, got to solve the mystery on our lonesome," she said, "and if we do, we can put our names on a shingle: 'Meister & Hahn: Dependable Detectives'" Eddie was more interested in the mystery of her body, but she quickly put a stop to that investigation.

"Have to earn that cheesecake," she teased, and slouching like a comic sleuth, she dragged him all around the cellar till they wound up back at the Ping-Pong table. Suddenly, she was so tired she let him ease her back onto it, handing him the flashlight, which he fumbled so its beam grazed the light socket overhead. They looked up at the missing ball she'd struck so hard it must have bounced up, wedging into the empty socket. "We've got our man!" she laughed. "But you get the girl later." When Eddie stretched up to coax the ball free, the lights came on again. He tried to get back to touching her but she ran for the stairs, blowing him a kiss.

Felix Meister was at the kitchen table eating Blini's pie for breakfast when Eddie came upstairs after a hard night on the narrow cot. Glad for a chance to talk about anything but his wife's cancer, Mr. Meister began interviewing Eddie about his plans for a career in pharmacy. Eddie was near convincing Mr. Meister that Gertie wouldn't want for much when she appeared with her mother's breakfast tray. "Pop, better get out of that undershirt, Ma's doctor's just pulled up the drive." When he mumbled something about being old enough to wear what he damn well pleased, she grabbed his arm: "Please don't embarrass me again by so much as whispering Dr. Russo's still wet behind the ears. And while I'm at it, I'm sure he heard you call him a hot-shot when I was helping him on with his coat last week."

Dr. Russo's biggest concern was not being able to control the pain and still keep Mrs. Meister lucid enough to engage in family conversation. "The thing of it is," he said, "she wants to hang on a while longer because, and I admit this is just a hunch, she's simply not ready to let go in spite of the pain and dread. I've found people in extreme distress will put off dying until something they've fixated on finally happens. Like the birthday of a loved one, say." Gertie and Eddie traded glances, both thinking wedding.

"Maybe we should just go through with it now," she said when Dr. Russo left. "You know, hire a justice of the peace and marry at her bedside. We don't have to bother with a rabbi. No one on our side of the fence will care. Besides, remember when uncle Jules stomped on the glass so hard it went through his shoe and bloodied his foot?" Mr. Meister managed a laugh, but all this wedding news was news to him, he protested, so they needed to catch him up on what was going on behind his back, he growled, arching his eyebrows for emphasis. And if that weren't enough, he was also unwilling to concede his beloved Anna was anywhere close to leaving him all alone.

"I mean, what if you do it and she dies right afterward or worse, during the doings. Want that on your conscience? Well?" he fairly shouted. "Besides, then we bury her and my life might as well be over, too." They tried getting him to understand the larger issue was her suffering; did he really want her enduring much more? Gertie was losing patience, Eddie could see, so he suggested she take a walk while he sat with Mr. Meister just to listen to whatever else he might need to vent at the moment

Gertie nodded. "Pop, I'm sorry. I know this is really hard for you, too. It's not like Mama's dead yet, so maybe we should take our time while we still have some. Let's hope, anyway." She whistled for Jake, her pet beagle, got her jacket and one of her mother's scarves, and leashed him when he padded in. "About time you get some decent exercise, old pal, been neglecting you. Let's go!" Jake pulled her out the door.

Eddie ferreted out a dusty bottle of brandy from the pantry, located two tumblers, and poured Mr. Meister and himself a healthy slug.

"'Here's to life', my pa used to say. 'Without it we are dead.'"

"That's pretty damn good," Mr. Meister said. "I can drink to that all right, even if it's not quite noon. Only met your father once or twice, at meetings of the Socialists at Steuben Hall it must have been, but I was impressed." Suddenly happy to talk about the past, Mr. Meister rambled on. "He had a way of gesturing, shaking a fist, poking his finger in the chest of anyone who challenged him, which, come to think, wasn't scary because he was a shrimp! But it was the sheer force of his arguments that swayed fence-sitters. I remember when he outfoxed the Communists we were having a furious debate with—one of those summer picnics by the lake that were supposed to unite us in common causes. 'Your country right or wrong,' he taunted them with. Something like that anyway. We were awfully sorry to learn he had to wind up in one of those so-called nursing homes. That can't be a whole hell of a lot of fun." Then he waved for more brandy, and soon they were both quite tipsy.

When Gertie returned, her father was trying to teach Eddie old Lithuanian drinking songs. Mr. Meister called Jake over, pulled him up by the ears to waltz him around, and promptly fell down on Jake, cracking his elbow. He started yelping and Jake joined in, while Eddie clapped wildly. Gertie banished Jake to his doghouse, told Eddie in no uncertain terms to remain seated until she tucked her father in, and when she came back downstairs she hauled Eddie down to the cot in the cellar to do his share of sleeping it off. When they'd sobered up by late afternoon, she had some news for them.

She'd spent the time they were clouded over sitting and talking more intimately than ever with her mother, who'd also been sorting out her own feelings. Mrs. Meister was suddenly so much clearer, so forceful about her wishes, perhaps because of her pain and anxiety and her dim prospects, that she persuaded Gertie she was right about what needed to happen next.

"I'll be fine for a while longer," she said, "and now you're spending more time together, have you thought of taking a little trip together? It's not a foolish romantic idea, Gittl. I've found going off where it's just you two against the world is as good a test as any to predict how you'll fare once caught up in tighter straits. While you're piling up the miles, if you look in on cousin Agnes, she'll not only put you up in style, you'll be doing me a special favor, help repair what's been something of a strained relationship with her. That would be Mama's dearest wish."

"Besides," Gertie said, pouring her father and Eddie some strong coffee, "Mama thinks I need to find out if the car I'll be co-owning is just a clunker, and its sorry owner a poor judge of quality."

"That's my Anna," Mr. Meister said, but slipped into his old concern that he might not be up to caring for her himself. Mrs. Meister had thought of that, too. Gertie and Eddie would stay until they could hire someone at least part-time to help out around the house, make sure Mr. Meister had decent meals and all. "I need to hear that from my Anna's own lips," he said, and went upstairs to see if she was still awake.

Eddie, who hadn't said a word, took the keys to the coupe out of his pocket and slid them across the table to Gertie. "If I were you," he winked, "I'd hire a good mechanic to get down and dirty on his creeper, slide under the body, and check out every blooming part before I signed on." When she asked him what a creeper was, he fell in love with her all over again, humming "Here Comes the Bride" to himself.

Once Gertie and Eddie had found a woman in the neighborhood, who was childless and bored sitting around the house, to help bathe Mrs. Meister, cook an occasional meal, and do some light cleaning, Gertie and Eddie packed to leave. It was a sultry day late in June. They were eager to beat the oncoming heat wave predicted to settle in over the whole mid-section of the country, the papers warned, so they climbed the stairs to Mrs. Meister's bedroom one last time.

They promised to send her some nice postcards for her collection, which an uncle had started her off on with a leather card he once sent from his Mexican adventures. Sorting through the cards, she had recently decided to make a project of pasting them into an album as a way of taking her mind off dying, which she said was awfully hard work of late. They flinched at the sight of the leather card she thrust at them.

"Is this what I think it is?" Eddie was clearly startled. The leather had darkened so he had to take it to the window to confirm the scene of an execution. Some cowboys stood under a tree looking up at a hanged man whose legs seemed to jerk, still in the act of dying.

"Oh, Mama," Gertie said with a tremble, "remember the last time you showed me this one? I was ten or eleven, and I threw up. That's a gruesome sight to send us off on."

"Well, Gittl, you're older now, aren't you, and I want you to remember how fortunate you are. On the road you're bound to see souls of all colors working in fields, and this sort of thing can happen to them at any moment. It doesn't take much for one man to kill another. I want to scare you because I'm not going to be there to protect you from now on. A mother worries, you'll find out I hope, when her child—and that includes you too, now, Edward—goes off for the last time." Her eyes fluttered and her legs started twitching.

"It's the damn blood gases going crazy again," Mr. Meister said from the doorway. He'd caught up with the conversation and realized she was in one of her apocalyptic moods. What she just means to say is she loves you so much she doesn't want any harm to come your way. That's all, isn't that right, my treasure?"

"Oh, is that what I mean, Mr. Felix Emanuel Meister? Well, well, Mr. Mouthpiece." She tried to go on but started convulsing. They all rushed to her side. Eddie took her pulse, Gertie and her father rubbing her arms. Then they pressed her legs gently down on the bed sheet until the cramps subsided.

"Small, hard, hopping a bit," Eddie said, his thumb pressed to her wrist, "but her pulse is coming around now, slowing down, more regular I'd say. Has she had episodes like this before, I wonder?"

Mr. Meister nodded. "Dr. Russo said it was blood gases, and to call him if she remained woozy for any length of time. Otherwise, it's more or less a normal pattern at this stage of the disease." They sat with her, watching her breathing even out, her limbs relax. Finally, she blinked when Gertie laid a cool cloth on her forehead, smiling the funny, sweet smile of one returning from a hard trail.

"Now where were we?" Mrs. Meister said. "Oh, I remember. You were telling me you're going as far away as it'll take you to test your limits, something like that, right? So bye-bye now, my children. Love each other the way we do." She looked over at Mr. Meister, who quickly exited so he could hide his tears. "And don't forget a nice postcard or two for my collection, which'll be yours one day. So be careful what you send!" Giggling like a little girl, she yawned and closed her eyes again. Gertie and Eddie joined hands, backing slowly out of the room, their eyes on her face until they closed the door.

"No tears now," Mr. Meister said when they kissed him goodbye at the curb, but he was the first to cry when Gertie reached out the car window to pick a thread off his bathrobe. He stood there, his hands behind his back trying to soldier up, his gaze following their hands, stuck high out the windows, waving back at him. He'd have stood there much longer if the woman they hired hadn't come along and said he'd better show her around, making quite clear she hated wasting time looking for things in a strange kitchen and all.

They almost didn't get out of Milwaukee that day because they decided to take the scenic lake road, only to find themselves stuck in traffic at the bridge over the bend in the river, just before the road swung south to Chicago. When they got out to mill with the other motorists standing around, to find out what was up, "the bridge is, dummy," some smart aleck cracked.

A cop sauntering along swinging his nightstick said, "You'll want to get a newspaper, folks, you're making history! Turns out there's a duck family nesting right under the bridge joints, and they don't want to close it or we'd have crushed duck for supper. So it'll be a while till they can coax the mama to give her ducklings a swimming lesson. By the way, they're starting a contest to name her so put your heads together. Gimbels is putting up prize money! Smart heads at the store must have realized what a publicity break's sitting right there along the bridge!" He took his cap off, wiped the sweat off his brow, and pointed up at Gimbels Department Store, which rose above the river.

When Gertie and Eddie got the map out and sat on a fender, looking for an alternate route, they realized they couldn't wiggle out of the line of cars without incurring some wrath. So like the other motorists they decided to relax, make a good time of it. Someone with a harmonica wheezed out some notes in the air, a couple took orders for pretzels and soda pop they saw a stand selling down a side street, and a little girl and her mother hopped on the roof of their car, starting to dance.

An hour later, the duck family having eventually been lured into the water by a bright soul who ran for a loaf of bread, tossing hunks into the water below the nest, Gertie and Eddie were waved across the bridge with the rest of the traffic. They could see the ducks paddling like mad along the far bank, lunging and plunging after more and more chunks of bread some gleeful kids were bombarding them with. By the time they cleared the main stream of cars turning every which way heading south, it was getting later and later. Eddie rubbed his eyes, guiding the wheel with one finger, making Gertie nervous. "I can't drive, you know," she said—he'd planned to teach her at one point but the opportunity slipped away—"so can we please turn off somewhere before we get caught up in any Chicago traffic jams, maybe get a bite to eat? I'm just about wiped out." She'd been feeding him pretzels to keep him going, but now she was famished. And maybe find a motel somewhere, is what they both were thinking, too.

"Good Lord," Eddie said looking at the gas gauge, "so's the coupe!" Just at that moment Gertie spotted a roadside diner south of Racine, its neon arrow pointing to a side road, its sign flashing MOTEL: VAC NCY. Eddie drove straight for the lone gas pump outside the diner. "Grab us a table while I fill her up and check the oil and tires.

After they'd polished off the meatloaf special, they ordered one piece of rhubarb pie in Mr. Meister's honor, with a side of cheddar cheese, and two forks. The waitress said that was a dead giveaway: they were either honeymooners, or on their last nickel. "On me, kids," she said. When Eddie said they'd remember her in their will, she reminded him that there wasn't a county law against tipping, and they shared a laugh.

"So, Ed, you were saying," Gertie mashed the crumbs with her fork, letting him lick it clean, "that you were ..." But she suddenly lost track of what she was going to say. Out the window night was falling fast. They fumbled with the Venetian blinds to let in the last of the light. The waitress came by for one last coffee refill. She said they couldn't spend the night in the booth, but if they wanted a decent bed her mother ran the motel back of the diner, with white-tailed deer and raccoons for company. "Honeymooners especially welcome," she chirped, and drew them a little map on the back of a napkin because it was tricky finding the office in the maze of cottages. "Just tell Mom Doris sent you," she said, going off to wipe the empty tables. Eddie called her back, realizing he'd need to get some change at the register up front. He didn't want her thinking he'd forget to leave a proper tip.

"Hell, Mister, in spite of what I said before, I'm fifty now and my mind's not exactly on tipping," Doris said with a suddenly weary look. Eddie was embarrassed he'd mentioned such a thing at all. Gertie, however, with her schooling in English—her best subject in high school—would recite Doris's comeback with great relish for years to come, stiffening up the way Doris had, pointing out the beautiful iambs.

And Doris was right about her mother's motel. The bed was not only decent, it brought Gertie and Eddie closer and closer. The next morning, on the way to the breakfast nook off the motel office, they squeezed past an older couple just leaving.

"Recommend the waffles with gooseberry jam," the portly, well-dressed man said with a twang. "Been coming here since before you were born, on the way up to our cabin on the Brule— great trout fishing if you ever get up that way!" he threw in. "Come here mostly for Mrs. Turpa's homemade jams, used to have them on sale, but she's getting on, alas." His wife giggled, pointing to his white hair, then to his belly. "So I guess we have to enjoy them on the spot; and I do my share slathering them on the waffles, French toast, pancakes, you name it!" His wife patted his arm, adding not to miss the nick-nacks for sale by the register. "And if you fancy old post-cards like Ethel here," he said, "there's not only a wonderful assortment, but Mrs. Turpa won't charge you an arm and a leg the way some antique dealers do." He pointed to several large wooden cigar boxes overflowing with cards and bowed in a natural, old-worldly way.

"Did you notice his polka-dot bow tie, Gert? My pa used to wear them by the dozen in the old days when he was tailoring for the high and mighty. He'd never stop mentioning the high point of his career: he was Eugene Debbs's all-time vest-maker. To his great disappointment I could never tie them to his satisfaction."

When Mrs. Turpa stuck her head out of the kitchen, they agreed to take the last two waffles on the griddle. While they waited, Gertie took a box of the old postcards down and started thumbing through them.

"Will you look at this one, Ed!" she said, handing him a slightly tattered card, one corner missing; with, he counted them, pictures of two dozen babies in rowboats afloat on a pastel sea, a faint whitecap breaking under the bow of each one. She let Eddie look his fill before she said, "Now turn the card over, see what's stamped and written on the back!"

"Babies in Boats/1901; Anonymous," he read. At that moment, Mrs. Turpa came through the swinging doors with their waffles, urging him to read the message aloud on what she said was her favorite card of all; one she'd never part with. "Ought to tape NFS on it," she said.

So Eddie began reading. The tiny, clear hand was easy to follow: "My Darling! Here are all the children I wish we could have, in their little arks, seas getting higher. And it'll be many a day before they get anything to eat again. But notice, my Love, that they don't seem to be worried at all. That's because they know our Lord will see them safely to shore. Till I have you safely in my arms again, yours in Christ, Hermann."

Mrs. Turpa crossed herself when Eddie finished reading, wiped her hands on her apron, and held a hand out for the card.

She said it was high time to preserve it under glass.

"You're right not to part with it," Gertie said, realizing she could never visit it on her mother anyway, for obvious reasons, and quickly picked out Moon Over Miami: soft, lemony wash of moon in a night sky clouding over yachts moored in a harbor. "Mama always wanted to see Miami, for unknown reasons. Just once before she had to go ahead and die, she'd say." They all broke into tears.

The Rehearsal

WHEN they reached St. Louis, the Mississippi, swollen farther north by earlier storms, was starting to rise, threatening to exceed flood stage, so Gertie and Eddie gave up on overnighting there with the idea of taking in some sights. Waving at the Arch, they inched along across the bridge, caught in a long line of traffic. "Onward, to the birthplace of the notorious Kansas City Kitty!" Eddie sang out. Once amusing, that moniker had stuck to Gertie throughout high school but lately she'd had enough of it. She swatted Eddie's knee so his foot came off the gas, and they nearly swerved into the railing, some angry honks from cars in both directions blasting their ears.

"I remember your saying it was much bigger," Eddie said when they finally reached Kansas City, easily found the house she was born in, and parked across the street before venturing out to have a look around.

"Well, I was much younger then. Everything was bigger, I guess." She led him through the still empty field next door, around toward the back. Delighted it still seemed a good place to play, she showed him how she and her girlfriends used to tunnel through the tall, lush grass. It was also where she used to trap the only pets they could afford in those hard times, before her father finished his butchering apprenticeship. Chipmunks mostly, but once a baby woodchuck that appeared abandoned, though her father finally convinced her to set it free again. "Pop said its mother would be heartsick over its absence, so I released it without tears for a change."

Watching her grow younger and younger before his eyes, Eddie was about to get playful and pull her down for a smooch in the grass; but she spun him around, suddenly took off, and was soon hidden from sight. After flailing around a bit, he finally hollered, "Can Gertie come out and play, please!" Sneaking up on him from behind, she blew the seeds and silky tufts all over him from the milkweed pod she'd picked and split open.

"It's snowing in July," she shrieked like a small child, letting him gather her up in his arms for a moment before she pushed away. "Only one thing wrong with this field now—no poisonous mushrooms. Mr. Bensman would be so disappointed." She'd been his most challenging student, and once called him out when he failed to identify a Death Cup a student had picked on a field trip and was about to sample. The principal gave Mr. Bensman a few days off to recover.

Gertie was leaning over the back fence, pointing to an upstairs window of the room she was born in, when a voice boomed out at them from a shed they hadn't noticed on the far side of the house. "Okay, who the hell are you, and what do you want?" A man in muddy overalls, one strap hanging down so his hairy chest bulged out, came toward them with a heavy wrench he made a point of hefting onto his shoulder. He had such a menacing look on his face that Gertie grabbed Eddie's hand and squeezed hard. They stood up straighter to give the impression they weren't hiding anything. Eddie shifted from one foot to the other, trying to stay calm until the man got to the fence and saw they meant no harm.

"Looks like you took a nice milkweed bath," the man said, reaching out with a beefy hand toward Eddie, who flinched, thinking a blow was coming. But the man plucked a tuft from Eddie's hair, and laughed, ""Whoa there, buddy, haven't killed anybody lately … Not since I left the force, that is. Broke my hip running down K.C.'s most-wanted, maybe you've seen my mug in the papers, is that it?" Gertie poured out her story so there wouldn't be more misunderstandings, which got the former cop to open the back gate. Waving them to follow, he ushered them up the back stoop to a kitchen under major repair, gave them some homemade dandelion wine, and said he really had to get back to fixing a busted pipe in the basement. "But take your time looking around. Once I wanted to get back to South Dakota where I was born, but they tore down the damn house before I got around to it. Not much family left either, so what'd be the point? But I'm happy to oblige you folks. Just hope you're not too upset with the changes I'm making. More's coming when I get a little stronger. The hip's still acting up. Don't recommend breaking one, but if you do …" Realizing he was carrying on, he stretched his leg out and rubbed it. "Just let yourselves out the front door when you've seen enough, but watch the third step from the bottom. Haven't got around to shoring it up yet. Sometimes I think I shouldn't have bought this place—too much for a divorced guy busy getting older faster than I thought I would. Like me and this goddamn broken hip. No kids though," he said heading back to the shed. "That's a relief."

Gertie looked as if she'd already seen enough, or at least heard enough, so when Eddie called her into the hallway to see a framed photo of Sgt. Erwin Findlay in the Kansas City Star of a few years back, grinning, hand-cuffed to "Moe Wurzel, K.C.'s most-wanted mobster," she shook her head and had to leave then and there.

The next point on the map they'd circled was Sedalia, where Agnes Stern, Gertie's mother's long-lost cousin, still lived. Her father had reconnected with Agnes after sending out notes about Mrs. Meister's illness to all the relatives in his assorted address books. Not only was Agnes still living in Sedalia when they started down Walnut Street looking for 4506, she was sitting on her porch. Eddie rolled down the window to get a better look at the number running vertically down the front post of her little clapboard cottage. When he called out, she stopped rocking and cupped her hand around an ear, shouting she was pretty deaf so they'd better come closer.

"Besides," she said when they got to the bottom step, "I don't bite and my dog's at the vet with worms." She put a shaky hand out to them and seemed to know who they were, seemed to be expecting them in fact, though she swore no one had called or written her they were on the way. Gertie suspected her mother had wired Agnes a few days before they left for Sedalia, but Agnes would hear none of that "conjecturing stuff," she called it. "Well, my cane's somewhere, but I forgot to tell it I'd be right back when I put it down," she giggled, "so I'd appreciate your helping me up if you want me to play a proper hostess." Rail-thin, her oval face set under a prominent widow's peak, she towered over Gertie and even had an inch or so over Eddie when they got her standing. "Got big feet too," she pointed down, and wiggled her toes in her open rubber sandals. "Time to paint the nails again, but it's hard to reach them these days."

When Eddie tried to make amends for staring at her, he got a little lecture about how she had just about put her anger to rest at all the clerks in town, who still kept asking her after years of waiting on her just how tall she was, anyway. She realized, when she recently hammered poor Mr. Ulrich with "big enough to beat the crap out of you," she'd better mind her mouth or life might get even harder to keep living.

"My mother wasn't quite as tall as you, Miss Stern," Eddie said plaintively, "but she got a lot of stares and comments too. Of all things, she used to say, from people who wanted her money."

"Well, first of all slide by the Miss stuff to Agnes, but don't call me Aggie. Makes me sound like some sort of athlete from one of those agricultural behemoths calling themselves universities, can you believe? Gertie, when your mother used to call me Aggie, I tolerated it if I was her guest, but not when she came to visit, which confused her. Well, we could just stand here going down my little list of grievances," she said, "but you'd be so bored you won't keep me company at the Fourth's festivities, which'd be a damn shame, because ours is one of the weirdest, most wonderful celebrations in the whole blooming state. But how about we go inside now and wet our whistles while you fill me in, Gertie Meister, on everything that's happened since I bounced you on my knee when you were, let's see, three, maybe?"

They paused to feel how long ago that really was. "How time flits," Agnes said at last, adding she was aware that for most people it flies, but not for the Stern side of her. Trying to recapture a moment of independence, she waved them on ahead into the house, but they wouldn't let go of her hands; and she seemed grateful they hadn't. Turning her around slowly, tall and shaky as she was, they walked her over to what was obviously her chair at the kitchen table: a high-backed Windsor with country lines which seemed made for her.

She gave Eddie precise instructions for mixing up a batch of mint juleps. "No wonder he's got the touch," she said when she learned he was a pharmacist in training. They drank to better times, and to Anna Meister's soul. Agnes had heard from Gertie's father now and then about Anna's struggle with cancer.

Each had a private moment filled with memories before Agnes finally said, "I'd better attach one of those earphones that's come onto the market. Normally I hate newfangled gadgets, but I admit it magnifies enough sounds so I can sort of get your meaning." She pointed to a shoebox up above the kitchen cabinet, and Eddie stood on a chair to fetch it. She unwrapped it carefully, as if it were a precious doll she was picking up from its crib after a nap. Gertie and Eddie watched transfixed as she strapped it on. They'd never seen or heard of the device. By the time Gertie finished summarizing the family's fortunes over the years, her voice was almost gone. "Anyone around the hard-of-hearing for a time, earphones or not," Agnes said showing them to the guest-room, "knows one's voice incurs a terrific strain for speaking up on a steady basis for any length of time. I am sorry about that!" Gertie and Eddie kissed her on the cheek and were about to add some words when Agnes gruffed, "Oh go on now, sweet dreams!"

They all woke up exhausted the next day, July 3. Especially Agnes, who wasn't used to so much company and chat. She said if she was going to be up for everything on the Fourth, at her age, she'd better stay in, close to bed. "Besides," she added, "I'm rereading Othello to see if maybe Desdemona doesn't get throttled this time. And I want you out of the house so I can have some peace and quiet."

After brunch, Agnes said the department stores in downtown Sedalia—"that'd be two," she held up fingers to underscore—were having their annual big, pre-Fourth fire sale. She pulled a $50 bill out of a fishnet bag that seemed stuffed with money, and said they'd be doing her an enormous favor if they bought themselves an early wedding present from her, so she wouldn't have to worry about sending them one on time. Her mind, she said, making a goofy face, was skipping a bit. She held her cheek nice and still while they kissed her. They said they'd try to stay out of trouble so she wouldn't find their names in the Police Blotter. She'd mentioned that everyone turned to it first in the weekly Sedalia Star. They had a good laugh at her favorite item of all: a few years back a local farmer was said to have lost "nine nice pigs somewhere off State Route 437."

Since Agnes lived only a mile or so from one end of downtown, Gertie and Eddie decided to stretch their legs. They soon found themselves slowed by an elderly couple walking right down the middle of the sidewalk in the European fashion, as if they were ice-skating. As Gertie and Eddie parted to skip around them, the man tipped his cap and the woman smiled. An image flashed in Eddie's mind, of the long, slow walks his parents used to take to the nicer neighborhoods, dreaming of owning a finer house one day. He was suddenly moved to cozy up to Gertie till he remembered she didn't like public demonstrations of affection, sometimes removing his arm from around her waist. A busy crossing as a pretext, he took her hand but didn't let go when they were safely on the other side. To his surprise, all she did was readjust the way he held her hand, moving his hand below and hers on top, then clamping down as if hers was the lid and his the pot.

The next thing he knew she was pulling him toward the window of a jeweler's, filled with a variety of molded hands, as if Rodin had dressed the window from his stock of sculptures. Mounted on little risers, the hands went every which way: curving up, cascading down, propped as if under a chin, pulling up a stocking; shaped like a rabbit's head, two hands joined at the forefingers and thumbs to suggest opera glasses—and all bedecked with jewels: sparkling diamonds of course, bright green emeralds; and one oddly shaped stone they couldn't identify. It was almost invisibly blue with a wax-like luster, and Gertie couldn't take her eyes off it.

They stood there for so long the door finally opened and a clerk who'd been watching them said, "Bring in your hearts and the collection's complete!" He bowed slightly, leading them to the vitrine where two other rings like the one she'd been admiring were displayed.

"That would be an onyx, Madam," he said unctuously, looking them over as if wondering whether or not they could afford it. "We don't get a lot of interest in this particular stone, but the women who choose it are," he cleared his throat, "well, they just know something the others don't, let me say." The handkerchief folded in his jacket pocket was drooping; he straightened it and tapped his fingers on the vitrine. When Eddie finally asked what such a ring might run, the clerk reached for a little key on his chain, unlocked the case, and with a flick of his finger turned up the price tag. He was not about to remove the velvet tray to offer a closer look. He seemed more and more convinced, from the way Gertie and Eddie traded glances, that the $195 price tag was way beyond their means; and he was right.

"Actually, we're just sort of looking, you know," Gertie said, "just passing through town. But we'll holler if we see something else, for sure." The clerk's smile had an edge, and when they turned toward the cheaper jewelry an aisle over, he called over a junior clerk to wipe their fingerprints off the glass. They made a pretense of seeming interested in a few other things, among them a brooch with room for a tiny photo between side clasps. Letting a decent interval pass, they called out thanks and left. The clerk didn't bother to respond.

Relieved to have exited, they caught sight of the department store Agnes had recommended as especially generous about returns. Just in case they bought something, she'd said, that bamboozled them once they were domesticated old marrieds trying like mad to understand the instructions for assembling. One reason she'd never married, they learned, was she couldn't find a man who could read instructions carefully, much less follow them. The store was no Gimbels; Sedalia was a small burg compared to Milwaukee. But it was laid out well: counters bright and clean; goods stacked in tidy piles; floors swept; genuinely helpful clerks who answered questions without pressure, giving one room to browse. "We've got to buy something, Gertie, anything," Eddie said, "reward them for knowing how to run a business." Just as he said that they passed the jewelry department, an artful poster hanging overhead: "His and Her Matching Silver

THE REHEARSAL

Wedding Bands — Will Last As Long As You Do — Have to Sell at $49 — You Have to Marry Just to Have Them on Your Finger / Sentiments Engraved Free on the Inside!"

An hour later, after they'd picked out what the clerk said was the classical Greek model, they decided to have them engraved, but not show each other the words they decided on till the moment they exchanged rings at the wedding. Having studied and fallen in love with Greek, Gertie actually wrote hers out in Greek, because the engraver said he could manage the script. Eddie built his around chemical symbols, so they were both in for a surprise if they made it that far.

Heading back to Agnes's cottage, the rings safely tucked away in their pockets, they held hands tighter than ever. "So," Gertie said, "what'll we do with the dollar in change?"

"That's an easy one," Eddie said, "we'll start a bank account for baby Jack or Jill, so if they go tumbling down they'll have something to fall back on."

When they got back, they found a note Agnes had left on the kitchen table in a flowing, cursive hand. She'd left them a cold platter with local meats and cheeses in the icebox, enough mint juleps for a sound night's sleep and some of her renowned apple cobbler, but begged their pardon for being out of whipped cream. "P.S." she'd added, "Unlike Desdemona, I'm merely sleeping. Hope you have earplugs. I snore like a tractor. P.P.S.: Tomorrow we light sparklers and sing Happy Birthday America!"

They were still asleep at noon. Agnes couldn't stand it any longer, so she knocked on their door. "And the dead shall rise!" she shouted and heard them stir. "Hey, lazybones, we should get to the fairgrounds early to see them setting up and all, that's half the fun." She put her ear to the door to hear feet thudding to the floor. "Not to mention stake out space on the little hill, the better to see the fireworks because it gets crowded fast," she said in her deepest voice. "People truck in from the whole county." Hearing nothing but silence again, she bunched up knuckles on both hands, hammering on the door. "I want you shined and gleaming, beds made so the quarter I toss on them bounces just so, or it's KP duty from now on. What do you think this is, summer camp?"

"Okay already," Eddie groaned. Even with her hearing going, Agnes heard him try to tickle Gertie awake, till she in turn threw what sounded like a shoe at him; and they began arguing, surprisingly angrily.

"Hey you two, you're not even married yet. Besides, there's no decent divorce lawyer in town," Agnes sang out, when she decided she'd just open the door and thrust her head in, which she immediately regretted. Stark naked, Eddie was sitting on Gertie, paddling her equally naked bottom, while she started screaming, banging the bed with clenched fists.

Thinking they must have played some troubling night music, Agnes said she'd leave them directions for taking the bus to the fairgrounds, and she'd go on ahead. "I'll be the only one for miles with a large, yellow parasol with blue dots; and, in case you forget what I look like, I'm basically a head taller than the rest of Sedalia. Assuming you've kissed and made up by then!"

Till early afternoon, Gertie and Eddie put as much distance between each other as the small cottage allowed. Eddie envisioned bussing separately to the fairgrounds and made his own copy of Agnes's directions. Those he slid under the bathroom door, where Gertie was taking her time splashing around in the tub, occasionally tossing off a phrase from *The Merry Widow* in her brassy alto. Eddie dropped to a knee for a peek through the keyhole, but she'd stuffed it with a blob of soap. When he said in a cutesy voice he'd be glad to steal a neighbor kid's rubber ducky, she threw something at the door. "Get me some smokes from my purse, and see if there's a beer in the icebox. Your crude rudeness will cost you more at the fair, and you will not hesitate to oblige.

THE REHEARSAL

Agreed?" she yelled.

He was already beginning to understand that if he obeyed her orders, they could march along through hill and dale without shots going off — to the next skirmish, anyway. If she turned sullen at unexpected moments, he'd start whistling nervously, with a look in his eyes of "why don't I just disappear into the woods and …" Then he'd recalibrate, realizing she was pretty pure of heart, more so than any other woman he'd tried and failed to find love with, even if he still didn't have the combination to her inner chambers.

They left the house for the bus stop in silence, though he did open the door for her, standing aside with a little bow while she curtsied past; and they boarded the same bus, though she asked him to sit behind her, which he was not unhappy to do: he loved looking at her from that angle. If you saw her turn around to share a look at the directions Agnes had written out — Gertie had stepped on the copy Eddie slid under the door, turning it to mush; saw the way she brushed his cowlick before she laughed at Agnes's precision; heard him sigh when she did; you'd say they stood as good a chance as any two humans of riding the same bus a long, long time.

There was nothing of a crowd yet at the fairgrounds, mostly just small groups of people assembling their booths. Gertie and Eddie stopped a moment to watch two guys working to set up the Dunk the Mayor venue. A few cops strolling around were jauntily swinging their nightsticks. A gaggle of girls, some sort of civic club, set up music stands in a gazebo big enough for a band and a dance floor; for the Sousaphones, a local group, the poster read, appearing for the first time in public. It didn't take long to locate Agnes, given her height and the yellow parasol. She was bobbing along near the food tables and waved when she caught sight of them.

You'd never have known what went on earlier at the cottage from the natural way they fell into conversation. Agnes spoke up first. "One of the highlights is the installation of Mary Alice Foster's own home stove. City workers haul it here from her kitchen, and plug it directly into the power source. That's that light pole over there," she said. "See that electrical box-thingy affixed? Soon as it's hooked up," Agnes went on, "Mary Alice starts greasing her pans with fresh-made lard to fry her famous fried chicken with all the fixings. It's not too soon to get in line, because hundreds of people will materialize just like that. If we dally, we'll not only go hungry, we'll miss the start-up of the parade altogether."

The truck bringing Mary Alice Foster and her stove drove right over the freshly mown field, and in a jiffy she and the stove were offloaded. The truck driver asked for her autograph, which she wrote on the bill of his cap with lipstick to cheers all around. Soon her lard sizzled in her pans, and, as Agnes promised, people with their noses in the air like animals following a familiar scent streamed from the nearby parking lots. When Gertie and Eddie mentioned they weren't particularly hungry, Agnes gave them some blankets she'd brought, pointed to the crest of a ridge, and said they'd better stake out a patch while she stood in line for some chicken to die for.

"But it's hours before dusk," Eddie protested. "What's the hurry? I'd like to walk around, try my luck at some games, see if I can still pitch a strike, dunk the mayor!"

Gertie nodded and said she was good at guessing which cup the penny was under. "My eye's faster than any sleight-of-hand carny guy," she boasted.

"Hey, who's the native here?" Agnes said. "Just get us some ground to watch from, then you can stroll around and make your fortune. No one'll touch our blankets if you spread them out but the wind, so make sure you weight the corners down with some stones. And if you don't check back soon, I'm eating all the chicken." She licked a finger. "Oh, just in case you win anything and would like to leave me a little house gift, I like teddy bears; but not those god-awful ones they dye pink and blue!"

To keep the tension between them to a minimum, Eddie deferred to Gertie's choice of spots to watch the fireworks from. When she finally decided on the perfect place, they waved back down at Agnes, pointing to where it was before splitting up to give time a chance to stop their spat in its tracks. They agreed to meet in an hour at the dunking booth, because Gertie said she'd like to see if Eddie still had that wicked fastball he used to strike everybody out with, except of course his best pal Schnooty, who crushed the last one Eddie ever threw, which crushed Eddie's teeth in turn when Schnooty got the sweet spot of the bat out before it whistled by. Before Eddie could get upset about being reminded of what was a lingering nightmare of a memory, Gertie slipped him a tender kiss. "I don't care whether or not your teeth are false," she cooed.

After poking around on their own for a spell, without having won so much as a cheap trinket, they found themselves on opposite sides of the main path through the grounds, divided by the first marchers in the parade, who were starting to fall in step behind the fire truck driven by Santa Claus. Eddie caught Gertie's eye across the way and mouthed, "Can you believe?" Gertie turned to a woman beside her, who said it was just another dumb decision by the excuse for a mayor and his stupid council, which only confused the children, not to mention being an obvious sop to the merchants out to make a lousy buck off any tradition, however holy.

Just then a man climbed up the ladder being extended from the back of the fire truck like some crazy tail. He straddled the top rung, sprayed his throat and shouted words into a bullhorn no one understood. "Oh," said a man next to Eddie, "that's the state senator. He's so drunk they'll soon get the net out they use to catch bodies jumping out of burning buildings, because he usually falls off at some point. The jerk claims it was intentional when he sobers up." Eddie looked over at Gertie, who was holding her hands to her face, clearly frightened the guy would fall to his death. Eddie made pitching motions to signal to meet at the dunking booth. She signaled back, and they extricated themselves from the ballooning crowd.

The mayor was climbing up onto the platform in his undershirt when they got to the booth. Two youngsters and an old granny were already in line, having paid their quarter to go to the mayor's favorite charity — the Sedalia Historical Society, the placard read. The first boy spit on the ball the attendant handed him, rubbing it in a practiced manner like a professional, Eddie pointed out. Winding up, rocking back and forth for an eternity, the boy finally let the ball fly, way up over the mayor's head, the back wall of the booth, and into the field beyond. Two dogs took off after it. Grinning broadly, the mayor leaned back in his chair, his hands cupping his knees. "If that's the best you can do, Mike Collins, you won't be pitching for your team much longer," he said, not recognizing the second boy in line, Mike's younger brother, who'd one day be the winning pitcher in the finals of the state's high school tournament.

Young Collins, even at age ten, was something of a phenom, though few knew of his gift at that time. He didn't do anything fancy at all. He held the ball out in front of him as far as his arm could stretch, squinted as if lining up a target to shoot at with his air rifle, slowly brought his arm straight back past his ear, and faster than your eye could follow, the ball struck the metal disk, plunging the mayor down into the ice cold water. He shot back up as if from a cannon and disappeared into a large Turkish bath towel. Minutes later, the attendant, to a chorus of boos, announced that the mayor had hurt himself in the fall. With great regret, he had to withdraw. The granny next in line cursed in what Gertie thought was German, while Eddie lamented he'd lost a chance to return to the big leagues.

At the booth next door that sold homemade brew for a quarter a cup, Gertie proposed a toast to the best southpaw never to have pitched a game in the bigs, and Eddie wasn't unhappy to touch cups with her. Catching sight of Agnes making her way up to their spot on the ridge, he said, "Chicken, my love?" Hunger had caught up with both of them, and they hurried for a taste of MaryAlice Foster's signature dish. They were licking their fingers when someone stepped up to the loudspeaker on the main stage in the center of the grounds. He thumped it several times to up the volume and said with a tremor in his voice that the weather would be changing fast. A storm, reportedly the next county over, would likely be on them in a short while.

Even as he spoke, wind came up, the sky turned lemon yellow, with a tinge of milky green farther out toward the west, and ominous clouds were getting darker and darker. Laced by lightning, they got everyone's attention, drawing some oohs and aahs and also some screams from parents at their children climbing the few trees around. Agnes's parasol, which she'd set on the blanket but hadn't closed, went cart-wheeling down the ridge toward a small pond, on the other side of which the fireworks' tubes had been lined up to be shot off like mortars after dusk. Several men of the crew made a dash for their truck. Some people with babies called it quits right then and quickly packed up to run for it. When the ring-toss booth was toppled by a terrific gust, two men struggled out from underneath, dazed if not badly injured. Half the crowd took that as a really bad omen, flooding toward the parking lot, objects flying out of their picnic baskets behind them.

Gertie and Eddie looked to Agnes for what to do. Her eyes were closed. She seemed relaxed, leaning back on her elbows, the wind undoing her hairdo. They exchanged worried looks but didn't utter a word. Neither did Agnes, for the longest while. Finally she said, "Could be a tornado Mother Nature's working on. She likes to bowl our alleys, nothing but buildings and a few trees in her way. We should probably take shelter in one of the storm cellars by the refreshment stand, but I'd like to enjoy the wind's force a while longer. At my age, I want more and more facts, especially where nature's involved. If you two are too worried, won't think the worse of you, promise. I'll meet you down there in a bit." She pointed to a line of people waiting to enter the shelters. Eddie wanted to hightail it, but Gertie rolled herself up in the blanket hard by Agnes's side, suddenly as relaxed as she was. Eddie couldn't make up his mind what to do. The wind helped him. It fell off just then to barely a whisper. Everything went dead still, so he calmed down, trying to hide how scared he really was. He remembered a freak tornado coming off Lake Michigan that took some lives north of Milwaukee when he was a boy. But the people running off in all directions now, he could see, stopped in their tracks, looked up, looked around, and then started off again in a more leisurely fashion, so he finally rolled himself up in the other blanket against Gertie's backside.

They were almost asleep, the fairgrounds all but deserted, when someone or something set the fireworks off on the far side of the pond. A rapid series of booming explosions rocked them wide awake. At first they had no idea what was what, until Agnes collected her wits. She pointed to the sky, filling with cascading colors as if pouring out of a gigantic fountain, punctuated by little bursts of white-hot light at unexpected intervals, accompanied by what sounded like ear-bursting pistol shots' but all so eerily pale in the late afternoon sky, presided over by a distant, silvery sun, that they couldn't tell where one color began and another left off. "It's raining sparks," Agnes whooped, "watch out!" She brushed a glowing ember off Gertie's hair. "I think we've just seen the grand finale," Agnes laughed, when the last embers fluttering down went out like fireflies turning their tail-lights off. As if the shoot-off had knocked out the impending storm, the sky drained and turned tranquil again.

Still somewhat dazed, they got up slowly, shook out the blankets; and brushed one another off, when Agnes spotted a line of tiny holes on Gertie's jacket where more embers had obviously landed. "You ought to donate it to the Historical Museum," Agnes said solemnly. "I'm prepared to deliver it to the mayor personally, when he recovers from his annual stupor. Of course, he'll make a show of demanding a full investigation." They sledded down the hill on their haunches, agreeing they'd seen something quite remarkable that would likely enter the annals of Sedalia's, if not the whole county's, Fourth of July celebrations.

The next morning Agnes sent them off with a huge breakfast and what she called a picnic basket of trip-eats, for the road west to they knew not where yet. There were tears about leaving much more than a distant cousin, but Agnes got on them for waxing sentimental. "Excuse me, but I've no truck for sentiments. How do you think this tough old broad made it this far?" she said, shooing them into the coupe. She sent them off with a steamship wave. Eddie didn't turn the key until she scooped up her cat off the porch and disappeared into the cottage. Gertie thought she saw her peeking out the window from behind the curtains as they pulled away.

Chekhov Inside Out

"Hank Deer, my pa's old Indian guide, once told me that if I took my new bride up to Lake Athapapuskow on a honeymoon, either she or I would not only catch a decent trout, we'd also remain married forever," Eddie said, moving Gertie's finger northwest on the map from Milwaukee to the lake's shape in Manitoba.

"Always wanted to see a Mountie in that cap and uniform up close," she said, tossing him the keys to his little coupe; "step on it!" By the time they got there they were down to pinching pennies to keep her in cigarillos and could afford only two nights in a tiny cabin a healthy walk from the shore. Black flies were out in such force that normal tourist business was way down, so the keeper threw in the use of a canoe and some basic fishing tackle. Eddie had no idea Gertie knew the first thing about casting so he gave her some tips as if she were a rank beginner while she batted her eyelashes, indulging him.

"You mean like so?" she asked when he handed her a rod, casting as if she'd just won a tournament. "Oh, I also remove the hook myself," she said impishly, jumping into the canoe, rigging his rod in a fashion he'd never seen, with a slip so the worm would float back up from the bottom when the weight sounded. He shook his head while she stripped to a velvety one-piece bathing suit she must have hidden somewhere because he'd have remembered it.

"Front or back?" she asked when he struggled to board the canoe without tipping it, cursing a halo of flies around his head. "By the way, you could market that perfume you gave me. See, no flies," she said cheerily, pointing to her breasts.

"You're probably a world-class canoeist too," he muttered, not sure if that was a sexual advance she wanted him to act on, and knelt in front when she slapped a paddle into his hand. It took some work before he caught on to her rhythmic stroking. After they'd managed to harmonize and see some of the main body of the lake, they agreed they'd better nose into a quiet cove. The sky was darkening, the wind picking up. Eddie was getting nervous, so Gertie said she'd save him if they overturned. One of the first things she learned after the judge declared them man and wife was he couldn't swim a lick. Asking her to show him the slip-sinker rig once again, he fumbled to get it right while she tied into the only trout the lake gave up that dark afternoon.

"You know I like it char-grilled," she said. "I'm going in for a swim now. The water's perfect, the way it usually is right before a storm." With that she knifed under the canoe, bobbing up on the other side when he finally caught sight of her. Then down she went again and disappeared until he had a nice fire going on shore, when she emerged from the surf like a mythical creature, her flesh glistening, her black hair torqued around her head, her hands trailing what she said were wild rice sheaths she'd tugged from the sandy bottom. "These will stiffen in the fire, be good to suck on if not smoke," she laughed, chucking him under the chin with one hand, while the other slipped down to his gonads, one of her favorite words he was coming to learn. Before he could say anything, she allowed as how there'd be no more "tricks" for a while, pointing to her belly. "There's a babe stirring inside, remember," she said with an edge.

They got through to her father to check on her mother when they found a Royal Canadian telegraph office with phone service in a small town south of the lake. Her father said Dr. Russo was running out of ideas, so he decided to take her mother for another opinion to St. Louis, where they could stay with family—yet more cousins Gertie had never met. An Egyptian doctor there was said to have developed a remarkably effective treatment for Mrs. Meister's cancer. "You two lovebirds just keep enjoying yourselves on your honeymoon. Soon enough you'll have your noses to life's grindstone," Mr. Meister said. "Not to worry, I'll be sure to call the number you've given me for the pharmacy in Utica if anything comes up. And, God willing, we'll look forward to seeing you when we see you, okay?" His voice, sounding almost worn out, brought Gertie to tears.

It was Eddie's turn to worry aloud about his father. "I'm not sure he'd recognize us at all," he said; and Gertie just nodded. They made a quick decision not to look in on him at The Elms, a nursing home in Buffalo, till they settled in Utica. Having just barely passed the pharmacy boards, Eddie had been nervous about his prospects when the offer came along to manage Hebring's Drugs & More, whose owner was recovering from a heart attack.

Gertie got the map out again so they could go over the various routes down to New York city before heading up to Utica to start his job. Honoring Gertie's side of the honeymoon-bargain meant looking up Aunt Fanny in Queens, who once visited the Meisters, and loved Gertie to death, who in turn started saying Aunt Fanny this, Aunt Fanny that till Mr. Meister said, "Enough already, she's your ma's wayward baby sister and will promise you anything from afar." Fanny had brought Gertie a souvenir photo of the Ferris wheel overlooking Coney Island. She'd point to the car poised at the top, whispering Gertie could see ships way out to sea from there.

Gertie persuaded Eddie to remain on the Canadian side of the divide till the last moment, instead of tracking south from Manitoba down through the States. The roads were rougher but gas, food, and lodging considerably cheaper, she argued, so they ambled along as far as Ottawa before dropping down toward the border — Ottawa only because she'd won a fifth-grade geography contest knowing it was the capital, vowing to visit it one day. "I still recall it derives from *ada-we*, a native word meaning to trade, taken from the name of an Algonquin tribe," she said. "And now that I think about it, that's likely the origin of my love for all things Indian."

When she leaned back, closing her eyes, Eddie risked sideway glances at her sudden calm. Once he tried to kiss her cheek lightly, narrowly averting a logging truck barreling along toward them, its load hanging way out into their lane. He hit the coupe's feeble little horn, which the truck answered with a blast of its own, jolting Gertie out of her reveries. "For a moment back there" — she was rattled — "I thought we were boiling inside the Great Kettle, which is what the natives called the falls above Ottawa." Eddie let his mind fill with visions of his own early days among the Oneida under Hank Deer's watchful tutelage.

When they reached New York they both agreed they'd remain two against the crazy world for now and not look up Fanny after all. Fanny had long complained no one ever bothered to visit her, though she'd once made the enormous effort, she'd remind them in mewling letters, to trek way out to Milwaukee. "We'll buy her a Coney hot dog if we cross tracks at the beach," Eddie said.

"Only if she recognizes me," Gertie said, which she knew was about as likely as seeing the Statue of Liberty strip to her bathing suit.

Making for a hot dog stand as soon as their toes dug into the burning sand, they decided to split one to economize, asked for one lemonade with two straws, and sat down on some chairs with yellow paint on them that hadn't quite dried. "Damn kids, must have tore the sign off," the stand man threw up his hands. Gertie calmed him down. She said their bathing suits had become instant art objects and would forever be treasured, which earned them a second hot dog free. They sat there for the longest time watching waves break, listening to the wind howl, whispering sweet nothings to each other, feeding the last crumbs of their buns to the gulls, and occasionally waving to other bathers who waved back. By nightfall they still hadn't tested the water, the waves darkening.

Finally, after the moon dimmed and not another soul was in sight except for an old gent snoring away under newspapers on a nearby bench, Gertie stripped naked. "I'll be back before dawn, Ed, and I'll need you here to wrap me in a towel before a cop comes along. Think of it as my first, maybe even my last, training swim for the English Channel. If anything happens to me ..." Cutting her off, recalling the tremor of fear he'd felt when she said one of her absolute intentions was to swim it in memory of Gertrude Ederle, after whom she'd been named, down to her middle name, Caroline, Eddie begged her never to say that again. Cradling his face in her hands, she kissed him on the eyelids and disappeared till dawn. Wrapping her in their only towel, he held her until she stopped shivering.

The only other thing Gertie wanted to do, before saying goodbye to Coney Island and moving to Utica, was ride the Iron Dragon. The papers said it was the year's prize ride at the carnival up the beach a stretch. Gertie even sacrificed several packs of cigarillos so they could keep running back up the steps to ride the Dragon again. Checking harnesses, they tucked their legs under the hood of their car and closed eyes for the flight the mind loves if other senses are secure. With each swing around, they swallowed smaller and smaller gulps of air. Eventually, they couldn't hang on tighter if they tried, with just enough reserves to make fun of each other's screams. When night fell smoke was added, which billowed from each car's nose.

On September 1, Eddie and Gertie met the Hebrings at the front door to the drugstore at exactly 8:00 AM, so they'd have an hour to look around the store and flat before any customers showed up. While Mr. Hebring, breathing heavily, inching his way along on his cane, walked Eddie around the layout, concentrating on the prescription counter and shelves of drugs, Mrs. Hebring took Gertie on a tour of the rooms in back, apologetic about the film of dust here and there, but proud of the sturdy furniture they were leaving behind. "We're helping you the way we were helped when we came to town," she said without so much of a thought that Gertie might have her own ideas about furnishing the flat, even if there wasn't an extra cent to do anything but make do with what the Hebrings were leaving behind—the proceeds Eddie pocketed from selling the family house after moving his father to The Elms were just about exhausted, and Gertie hadn't entered the union with any sort of dowry, given her mother's ballooning medical expenses.

Gertie tried to show some gratitude to Mrs. Hebring, even though her heart wasn't in it—she couldn't imagine gravitating to Grand Rapids modern at any age. Just before saying goodbye, Mrs. Hebring turned teary. "You know," she said, "we never did have to fix up a room as a nursery because, well, we tried and tried to get pregnant, but I hope you'll figure out what to do if you're fortunate enough to raise a family here." She looked around wistfully and on a sudden impulse gave the beaded, fringed lampshade over the dining room table a twist, watching it swing around before slowly moving back into place.

Gertie took both of Mrs. Hebring's hands in hers and said she just knew she'd have been a wonderful mother. If Mr. Hebring hadn't called out, "Bea, Beatrice, time to wipe our tears away and just leave," she looked as if she might sit back down, not move for a long, long time.

After the Hebrings left, Eddie fussed with some displays, making a note to redo one of the front windows, then took a moment to look in on Gertie just before opening for business. She was exploring a cabinet she'd not noticed earlier and shrieked, so he came running. "Good Lord, Ed, lookie here!" Together they counted seventeen bottles of various whiskeys, Scotches, ryes; and even a few fancy liquors at various levels of consumption.

To a bottle of anise-ale, Mr. Hebring had attached a note: "For good times and bad, but may those be few and far between!" Gertie talked Eddie into a quick toast to the Hebrings, as well as their own fortunes, so they started in on a half-full brandy bottle, almost managing to kill it, Eddie thinking he'd better not lean over the counter too far in the direction of a customer.

"Okay, Ed, off to work with you, bring home some bacon while I get our quarters spick and span by the time you close up, clear the registers, and let's hope at least the coin drawers are nice and full by then!"

Numbers of customers came by, curious about the new pharmacist and all, looking around for any other changes, and taking their time introducing themselves, but it was a slow sales day. When Eddie pushed the clear-button, cranking the arm on the side of the main cash register, just $47.49 popped up on the little metal dollars-and-cents tabs behind the glass panel at the top. He loosened the bow tie he'd taken to wearing in school, hung up the cream jacket Mr. Hebring had left him, and stepped out onto the street for some air. It was misting. He tilted his head back, shut his eyes. It was nine-thirty, and the little restaurant next door had already closed for the night. Across the way at the fire station a man was hosing down the lone engine.

When he heard a noise behind him in the store, Eddie came back to himself. Gertie was casting the red sweeping compound on the floor and looking for the push broom. She shooed him away. "My dogs aren't as tired as yours, flatfoot," she teased, so he took a stroll around to familiarize himself more with what was where, hopping over the broom when she swept past. At the display window, his hand moved out to the switch. The lights went out, then they came on again; they'd pulse all night long, and Gertie and Eddie drank to the clever old Hebring's timer-device before sitting down to Mrs. Meister's bean and barley soup recipe, which Gertie was determined to get right by and by. Without saying much, doing the dishes together, they soon called it a night during which they slept side by side but did not move toward each other till morning.

Business picked up when schools opened toward the middle of September, later than back home where they'd grown up, because orchard families needed help from their kids to bring in the last of summer's fruits. "Had seven so I wouldn't need no hires," Ninian Sutt said one night when he stopped by just before closing for his weekly ration of rum-soaked cigars and Eddie chatted him up. Sutt owned one of the largest orchards around. "Course," he coughed, "if I don't kick this filthy habit they'll inherit the damn place sooner than they'd be ready for it." He just laughed when Eddie said he'd fix him some syrup to clear his lungs before the cough tore one out. Eddie came out from behind the counter and turned Ninian Sutt around so he could put an ear to his back when he told Sutt to cough. He had to stretch because Sutt was fully a head taller, and so large across it was hard to hear into his lungs even with the soda glass Eddie pressed against him, his ear glued to the bottom for louder listening. When he asked Sutt about the nature of the cough, Sutt just said, "Hell, Hahn, I got good inhale but poor exhale." A bit alarmed, Eddie said maybe he'd better see Doc Gussow right away, above the bank. Sutt just shook his head, picked up his change from the little rubber mat on the tobacco counter, and used the spittoon in the corner on his way out.

In late October, Mr. Hebring's wife wrote that her husband's recovery was bumpier than expected and though Eddie had signed a contract for a year, it seemed unlikely that Mr. Hebring could return at all. Things were going well until a letter arrived from Mr. Meister, who implored Gertie to come right home. Mrs. Meister had taken such a turn for the worse that even the Egyptian physician they'd consulted agreed the end was near. Gertie's hands shook as she handed the letter to Eddie, who readily agreed she needed to be on the next bus. He assured her that if he couldn't handle things—Gertie had taken to clerking at the perfume counter and in notions when Eddie advertised special sales to drum up more trade—he'd look for part-time help so he'd not get sick from exhaustion.

"If I get really lonely," he said, "I mean if you have to stay on for any length of time, maybe I'll get us a dog. Ninian Sutt's giving away a litter of springer spaniels, I hear. He says they make fine family pets, and if I'd need a pheasant to add to the larder, a spaniel's the ticket."

Gertie threw her arms around his neck, almost knocking him over. She'd been thinking of getting a dog to keep her company. They'd both understood, going into "the venture," they called it, that he'd have to keep long hours to build the business, quite apart from being able to put something aside for fixing up a nursery now that Doc Gussow confirmed they were really pregnant.

Just before the bus pulled away, Gertie opened the window. "If a healthy female's available in that litter, Ed, name her Peggy, you hear?" Eddie recalled she'd once had, and lost, a mutt named Peggy. Nodding, he blew her a kiss.

The first week Gertie was gone Eddie practically lived in the store till Ninian Sutt's wife said he looked like death warmed over and promptly brought him a scalloped-potato casserole, which temporarily revived him. "Our oldest girl, Louisa, would gladly help part-time if things pile up on you, Mr. Hahn. She's our most dependable, sociable child. I don't have to tell a smart man like yourself it wouldn't hurt to have a clerk most of the town knows. She wouldn't need to be paid top-dollar, be worth every penny, or our name's not Sutt."

When Louisa reported extra early for work the following Monday, Eddie had to look up at her, too. She had her parents' height and their orange hair as well, surrounded by a sweet if goofy smile, which with her lisp held your gaze, as if you expected her at any moment to turn into a princess and step out of her gawkishness. Eddie plied her with a long list of instructions before setting her up behind the soda fountain, repeatedly asking her to write things down. She refused, but totally won him over when she proved she remembered everything. Finally satisfied she'd work out fine, he stressed pushing the large size of anything, from toothpaste to hair oil, being careful not to dish out too big a scoop of ice cream, and going easy on the chocolate jimmies. She didn't hesitate letting him know, then and there, that was against her religion. He tried insisting that buying the large size would save customers money in the long run, but she was firm about giving folks what they said they wanted, period. He didn't protest further or risk threatening he might have to let her go if she wouldn't do things "the boss's way," as he'd been taught. Gertie's efforts to get him to back off in the face of superior argument was beginning to make a difference. In a recent letter to her, Eddie joked about the progress he was making listening to others, especially strong women; and he included a picture of Peggy, who wasn't housebroken yet but taking solid food if he mashed it up just so. He also mentioned that though Peggy was content to gnaw on a baby blanket in her box most of the time, he'd taken to carting her back and forth between the flat and the store. In other words, between Peggy and Louisa he was holding out pretty well in Gertie's absence, though he drew a sad face, exaggerating its down-turned mouth, at the end of the letter.

Dr. Russo was at Mrs. Meister's bedside when Gertie arrived. When she came up the stairs, he stepped into the hall, putting his hand lightly on her shoulder. "There's nothing we can really do at this point," he said quietly, "except make her as comfortable as possible." Gertie had tried to prepare herself for the worst. She'd almost forgotten to change buses in Chicago, caught up as she was in a litany of mostly cherished memories, even as she ran over all the times she knew she'd let her mother down. Her mother, of course, never let on that her darling was anything but quite perfect, which only exacerbated Gertie's regrets. Trying to focus on what Dr. Russo was saying, she caught a glimpse of her mother's favorite, ancient pink nightgown behind him, heaped up on her body, her head cut off by the angle of the bedroom door, and she fainted.

Gertie woke up in her mother's little sewing nook, her father and Dr. Russo kneeling by her side, fanning her. Felix Meister had been in the cellar driving nails into a board. He'd start out with a pattern in mind, then just give up and pile-drive all the nails in sight right through the board, for good measure banging his thumb when his despair got the best of him. The first thing Gertie noticed was a bandage on his hand. Once, terrified, she had watched him through a crack in the cellar door—his twin brother had died suddenly—hammering away at his workbench. "Oh Pa, oh Pa, I'm worried about you, too," she said, taking his head into her lap when Dr. Russo returned to Mrs. Meister's side. "Come on, Pa, let's have a nice cup of tea with a spot of that fine old cognac you've been saving forever, okay?" Dr. Russo managed a weak smile, said he'd join them on his way out just as soon as he upped Mrs. Meister's dose of morphine so she wouldn't rouse in the middle of a spasm, getting drenched in the terror of it all.

Once Gertie got past feeling overwhelmed by anything, she had an uncanny ability to re-focus and go on with renewed purpose and energy. So when Dr. Russo was about to leave she held him back a moment. "I don't want to wake up one morning with Ma dead beside me," she began. She'd already decided she'd sleep on a cot at her side. "Isn't there some sign we might have that the end was near?"

Dr. Russo lit up. "Funny you should ask. My Egyptian colleague, who examined your mother in St. Louis, remember, has a fascinating theory about predicting time of death ..." He stopped mid-sentence, sorry to be putting things so crudely when he saw Gertie blanch, but she begged him to continue. "Well, Dr. Mahoud says if you give patients simple arithmetic problems, nothing too hard mind you, they should be able to solve them fairly quickly if they're stable. Something like two times three, or even just two plus two. Twice a day, once when they wake up in the morning, then again right before tucking them in at night. If they can't answer, Dr. Mahoud's found that death's quite imminent. That sounds crazy, and of course he's the first to admit it's hardly a scientific theory. On the other hand, he's had a long, distinguished career and has treated many patients." Dr. Russo apologized again, but Gertie couldn't have been more grateful.

The very next morning Mrs. Meister woke to the cool cloth Gertie pressed to her forehead. She smiled, her lips forming a little kiss when Gertie dabbed her wrists with a spot of jasmine perfume Eddie had taken to sending. Ever so slowly she lifted a wrist to her nose to enjoy the fragrance. "Ma," Gertie said, "first sip a little juice here, then we're going to play school the way we used to before you packed me off to first grade, remember?" She waited for her mother to catch up to her meaning. When she finally seemed to understand, nodding the slightest nod, Gertie began giving her doses of arithmetic—that morning, again that night, and for the next week or so. When she couldn't quite say the answer, she lifted the correct number of fingers to all the little problems, so Gertie and her father were able to get some sound sleep, trusting more and more in Dr. Mahoud's theory as the days passed.

Then one day, for unknown reasons, Gertie upped the ante. Perhaps she was just bored, or on a whim wanted to see if increasing the difficulty of the problems would actually strengthen her mother. Some part of her might have tried going Dr. Mahoud one better, adding a corollary to his theory. That day Jonathan apples put in their last appearance at the fall farmer's market—they were the only sort Mrs. Meister would use to put up applesauce for the winter. Gertie rose early to make sure she'd have the best selection and on impulse bought a whole crate.

Exactly a hundred apples! She was so astonished she forgot everything else and bolted up the stairs to tell her mother, who was drifting in and out of sleep. Ma, I just bought the last of the Jonathans at the market to make you some nice applesauce, remember how much you love it? Well, just for fun I started counting. When I got to ninety-nine, I saw one more in the corner of the crate. Now, how many does that make: ninety-nine plus one?"

Mrs. Meister raised herself up slightly, holding onto Gertie's arm. "Wait, wait a minute," she seemed to say. "I know the answer. I'll have it in a second, you'll see. Such an easy one ..." Suddenly she sank back down, her face drew sweat. Feverish, she lay there searching for the answer. Time stopped. She started to tremble. Gertie was ready for this moment in her mind but not her body, and she trembled, too. Finally, her mother's eyes cleared, her body relaxed. "I've got it, Gittl, it's a hundred of course, think of that!"

Gertie hugged her, their heads nestling together. Then she wiped her mother's face and helped her sip a little water from the glass by the bed. About to leave, but like an actor who turns around in the doorway for one more word, Gertie said, "Ma, those hundred apples, remember? Well, what if we took one away, what then? A hundred minus one, how many is that, Lovie?"

Again, the little scene played itself out. At first, Mrs. Meister fell back on the pillow, shuddering. "Easy, that's such an easy one," Gertie thought she heard her say. It seemed as if an hour had passed when Mrs. Meister's eye brightened and she whispered, "I don't know that anymore." And died.

To the horror of the religious community, she left instructions to be cremated, even though the rabbi warned of God's anger; it was decidedly against His Law, and she would have trouble explaining herself to Him.

"She didn't want to take up any room, simple as that," Mr. Meister said, "even though we have two plots under a nice shady tree at Spring Hill. She said my next wife could have the other; and she wasn't joking, either." He couldn't stop the tears from coming.

"Why couldn't I go first?" he kept saying to Eddie when he arrived, having left the drugstore in Louisa's care and come by bus because the coupe needed a major overhaul. Doc Gussow had promised to stop by evenings to fill serious prescriptions; but Eddie was tense about a number of things, Gertie could tell. At first she thought he might be worrying about his own father. Clearly, from his mood and manner, something else was on his mind, which Gertie decided to put off investigating until they boarded the bus for Utica again.

They were able to leave right after the service, because Mr. Meister woke up with the same fierce clarity he'd passed on to Gertie at an early age. An amateur boxer at one time, he said he couldn't wait to get knocked down so he could shoot right up again, come out swinging in the next round. So when he insisted he could care for himself, that they'd better leave or he'd put them to work fixing the porch swing for starters, Gertie and Eddie knew they could take him at his word. "Now scram, you two, you have your own lives to lead. I'll write once a week but only if you write back, understood? Now git, Gittl! Get it?"

"Do we git it, Ed?" she said imitating Mr. Meister's voice.

"I think we definitely do git it, Gittl," he said.

"Oh my God, what have I set in motion?" Mr. Meister kept repeating, rolling his eyes, till they shut him up with hugs.

Eddie didn't have to ask Gertie if they might stop off in Buffalo on the way back to Utica to look in on his father at The Elms. She'd long assumed they would do just that, adding they needed to ponder whether or not down the road it was a good haven for her father as well.

They could hardly believe their eyes. Emanuel Hahn was practically running The Elms; like a little Napoleon, he himself joked, sticking his hand inside his self-made vest for effect, thrusting his head out sideways, his albino-white hair tinged with a bit of black shoe polish, he was quick to admit.

Having taken to staging little plays in the main lounge, he claimed they were written by forgotten Hungarian playwrights whose work he'd kept alive in the back of his brain. "And wonder of wonders," he said, when he introduced Gertie and Eddie to a Mrs. Holman at lunch, "Harlene here is an amazing talent! Not only has she returned to the land of the living, she's starring in my productions." Her face flushing, Mrs. Holman excused herself to use the powder room. Not uttering a word—Gertie and Eddie exchanged glances, as if to say "don't ask anything"—they sat there waiting patiently for her to return. Eddie's father sprang to life again when she did. "Harlene," he said, taking her hand, motioning them all to repair to the lounge, "would also make an unforgettable Hedda Gabler, don't you agree? But my little company needs more training before biting that one off."

Straightening her skirt, then fussing with the seam of a stocking on the back of her leg, Mrs. Holman said in a voice a critic would call theatrical, "Your father and I see eye to eye on most things, except for hominy grits, or what he calls 'bastard

Kruska,' which I find revolting and refuse to eat anytime, never mind every morning. And he'd best have the original play to hand, not his supposed translation, if he wants me to swallow that one!" When she laughed, she threw her head back, touching a hand to her ghostly pale throat. Then she and Mr. Hahn launched into a detailed discussion of a future project she seemed to be designing sets for. As if Gertie and Eddie weren't present at all, Harlene Holman and Emanuel Hahn traded notions back and forth like excited adolescents about how to portray and sequence everything in Chekhov's plays that takes place off-stage, especially the duels. "Chekhov Inside Out is what we've decided to call the production, don't you think that's catchy?" Mrs. Holman said to Gertie in passing. "And perhaps you could write drama critics of the leading papers in your idle time. We'd set aside front-row seats for any able to attend. For what's sure to be the talk of the season, won't it, Emanuel?" she said breathlessly to Mr. Hahn, who beamed, patting her hand.

Gertie's and Eddie's goodbyes fell on deaf ears, as Mrs. Holman and Emanuel Dearest, as she addressed him, never stopped looking into each other's eyes. When Eddie announced they had to make a run for the last bus to Utica, they just nodded, holding out cheeks for a peck. "I guess that crosses pop off the worry-list for a while," Eddie said to Gertie, who suddenly seemed in some pain when she slid into a seat on the bus and leaned her head against the window.

"What is it, my Love?" Eddie looked anxious.

"The last sprint for the bus wasn't too smart, Ed. I think I might have broken my waters."

Putting his arm around her, he drew her gently to his shoulder. "Well, let's just go real easy from now on, babe." Needing to stretch out to ease her back pains, Gertie asked Eddie to take the empty seat between them. The closer they got to Utica, the more Eddie realized he couldn't put off much longer the matter of the wicked rumors about Louisa and him which had surfaced and begun to circulate. He'd tried putting two and two together to the point of exhaustion when the call came to hurry to Mrs. Meister's funeral. Some nasty-minded customer had seen him feed Louisa's bastard child an ice cream cone in front of the drugstore, while she smiled at them through the window. The boy, worrisomely slow for his age, had suddenly thrown his arm around Eddie's neck, saying something like "Daddy, Daddy, me a big boy, me eat more ice cream with lots and lots of sprinkles, Daddy," loud enough for the whole block to hear. No wonder Eddie had arrived at the Meister's looking like he'd been to hell and back.

But what he did instead, when Gertie jostled from her nap because the bus driver had taken a wrong turn, suddenly throwing the bus in reverse, was tell Gertie some nice news first. "Can't wait to see how you and Peggy take to each other," he began, taking some time to describe how the spaniel's looks and behavior had already changed in the short time since the Sutts had delivered her. "And then there's good old Doc Gussow telling me he's delivered almost everybody in Utica by now, so if you dare seek another midwife—that's what he calls himself—he'll slit a wrist and it'll be your fault. I admit that turn of mind could upset any mother-to-be, but in the short time I've filled his prescriptions and talked to his patients, well, I've come to respect him a whole lot. Besides, he helped get the hospital up and running when he first came to town. The word is the whole staff there, from chief nurse to janitor, darn near adore him. So I'm hoping you'll take to him, too, though of course it's your call, Mother."

"Good Lord, Ed, I hope that's just a bad joke!" Gertie suddenly sat up straight, fixing him with a cold eye. "Only if you were Abe Lincoln would I let you call me 'Mother,' which Mary seemed not to mind, I'm sorry to say. My own dear mother stopped my equally dear father in his tracks the first time he called her 'Mother.' I'm not only not your mother," she said more sharply, "if mothering is what you want I want out right now!" Eddie clammed up the rest of the way.

It was late Sunday night when they reached Utica. The store was long closed, but Louisa and her mother, who'd come by to help tidy up the flat in back—Eddie had left in a hurry and things were a bit of a mess—still busied about. Eddie stumbled through introductions, sensing the swirling rumors were also having an effect on Mrs. Sutt. She looked grimmer than Louisa, if seemingly grateful Eddie was back—to share the discomfort, he told himself. He also feared they'd assume he'd already told Gertie about the rumors and might say something before he had a chance to talk to her in private. If she found out from anyone but him there'd be hell to pay, he thought, even though he had little grounds to think that of Gertie. He simply tended to fear the worst when it came to his own lapses. Mr. Hahn's belt-whippings, infrequent though they'd been, were never far from his mind whenever he'd not done what he should have, at least not soon enough.

Gertie came to the rescue; twice over, it turned out. First, she was really exhausted from the journey, not to mention brooding about her mother's death, and hardly able to play hostess. Even at that late hour propriety might have called for insisting the Sutt women stay for tea, but Gertie simply said bed was where she needed to be, inasmuch as she was pregnant and didn't want to risk the health of an unborn on top of all else that had come their way.

"Clarity is a blessing," Mrs. Sutt finally said when she recovered from Gertie's shocking announcement, as she put it to her husband later on, while Louisa gave a little jump for joy, pulling her mother out the door. Eddie called out after her that she deserved a few days off, and he'd see her mid-week, knowing he'd need the time to walk Gertie through the thicket of rumors.

Having risen early but rested for a change, they were enjoying a leisurely breakfast when Eddie decided it was high time to broach the subject. Not only did Gertie not suspect anything had ever gone on between him and Louisa, she was outraged Eddie didn't immediately confront the man he suspected of having started the whole nasty business. Eddie soon gave up protesting the guy might have been innocent, because she said all over again, "So what, he could have denied it but at least notice would have been served for the whole town to hear. Furthermore, it might have died a sudden death, then and there, Edward Emanuel Hahn! It's not as if he'd have challenged you to a duel. Where's some spine?" Then she simply walked out to the back porch to meet Peggy, forgotten about till that moment.

Peggy was timid about venturing out of the little doghouse Mr. Sutt had thrown into the bargain, barely sticking her nose out to sniff Gertie's hand when she bent down to look in. But after one look at Peggy's eyes, one brown, the other red — there'd been a full albino in the litter — and the white ruff around her sleek neck, and the tan fringe running off her coat and footpads, Gertie was smitten. Finally, Peggy had the good sense to lick Gertie's hand.

"Now here's what we're going to do about Louisa, her poor little lad, and us to boot, Ed," Gertie said when she returned to the kitchen, Peggy tight on her heels. "Get us a blanket. This girl, I've got a hunch, will want at least half of it." Looking down at Peggy, she stroked her bony head. "And we'll meet you on the couch." When Eddie looked at his watch, Gertie grew annoyed. "So you'll open the damn store ten minutes late, Ed. I'm here to save your reputation, and mine as well, bud. Now fetch us that blanket, we're cold!" As if on command, Peggy wagged her tail and Eddie did as he was told.

"You and I and a still very unborn whoever's in here," Gertie said, pulling his hand to her midriff, "and Louisa and her boy are going to the circus. Ringling Brothers is coming to town, with musicians, jugglers, clowns, high-wire artistes, elephants of course, lions and tigers too, and let's hope some able trainers!" He started laughing. She'd almost memorized the placards they'd seen in shop windows when the bus rolled into town. "Get it? We appear en masse at the most public event of Utica's otherwise dismal year and poof, there go those rumors I guarantee you. Louisa and her kid, not to mention her parents, are even worse victims in a way." Gertie patted the couch beside her and down Eddie plopped on the other side of Peggy. "Your job," she said softly, "is to convince Louisa and her parents that it's a good plan for them, too." Then they heard some knocks on the front door to the store. "Early customers, likely," she said, shooing Eddie out to open up and giving Peggy's ears a good scratch.

Two Saturdays hence they climbed aboard the Sutt's tractor-trailer bed and sat down on old, soiled cushions next to Louisa and Earl, her slow little son, while her parents sat up front. Mr. Sutt's beefy hands a match for the wheel, they rumbled out of the barn headed for the fairgrounds. Gertie had a way of drawing out other women so she soon had Louisa sharing intimate details of Earl's problems. He'd come into the world with a tumor on his spine, six toes on one foot, four on the other, just for starters. There'd been two years of multiple surgeries before anyone ever noticed his brain wasn't quite right either. At that point, Gertie reached out for Earl, and he crawled right into her lap, all eight years of him, though he looked four or five at most. Gertie then took over for the rest of the route, telling Earl all about Peggy, promising to introduce them. When he made some agitated noises Louisa had to translate. "He says he knows all about Peggy already because he saw her being born." Gertie had forgotten about Peggy's origins.

Being born, being born," Earl stammered, shaking his head vigorously, smiling with half his face. He looked up and patted Gertie's face as if she were Peggy. Then he made a private joke Louisa tried to decipher. It seems he had a notion that if they watered the elephants they'd get in free, she said. She had no idea where he sometimes got his ideas but some were downright pleasurable, she said with great pride.

Eddie had managed to get discounted tickets through a customer for whom he'd reduced the price of a costly prescription. The big top that Ringling used for the Utica engagement was not as large as some they erected in bigger cities, so although their seats were in the last row, right under the top's cowl and they had to look around a couple of poles, all three rings were quite visible. Earl immediately started laughing before they all sat down, pointing to a goat sucking milk from a bottle while serenaded by a seal playing a horn a clown held to its snout. He kept laughing so hard, nodding his small head, that Louisa put her hand over his mouth till he stopped, while people entering the row looked them all up and down. Eddie thought he heard one guy say something about what a queer family the Sutts had turned into. Ninian and his wife just smiled at the guy edging past to his seat who would have stepped on Earl's foot if Louisa hadn't spirited him up into her lap. Gertie whispered to Eddie that if she weren't pregnant she'd spill some lemonade on the guy at some point — he wound up sitting next to her — when he was distracted by the clown act unfolding in the center ring.

Soon the ringmaster appeared, animals were led out to a drum-roll, and the whole tent roared to life. Earl got so dizzy looking back and forth from one ring to another he lost sight of an aerialist on the high bars who swung out at one point right in front of them, waving right at Earl with a free hand. Eddie hollered out loud to please do that again, taking Earl from Louisa's lap to point him in the right direction. The highlight of the whole show for Earl, he tried to dive out of Eddie's arms toward the high-flyer. Eddie had to use all his might to restrain him; and quickly passed him to Grandpa Ninnie, as Earl called Mr. Sutt, who kept Earl firmly between his legs till the last fanfare sounded and the tent began to empty.

"In the end," Earl suddenly shouted out to half the grandstand, "big cats do what they get trained to." All the Sutts applauded, unaccustomed as they were to hearing him cobble together a whole sentence, much less so clearly. However, when no one from those leaving from the rows below turned to acknowledge him, Earl's face fell. Half extending his arms, he reached out to Gertie. Then he broke into a singsong verse of his own making: "It isn't for us to say how people come to play, dadah, dadee ..." He waved to the last of the people trailing out of the tent, some of whom, Eddie realized, had gossiped about Louisa and him, and he almost gave them the finger.

"Wish you had," Gertie said. She'd taken Earl by the hand, helping him jump with great glee down the plank seats from row to row as they descended, the Sutts exchanging grateful looks. They were among the last stragglers to exit the big top when Earl pulled on Gertie's hand to stop. They looked up where he pointed. The lights were going out all around the tent; and Earl said, once again so distinctly it was nothing short of miraculous, "Well, they are very poor people. I keep mine on all night!" Pale, suddenly serious, he reached for Louisa's hand while hanging on tight to Gertie's, and walked them into the sawdust in the center of the ring. "I'm one of the animals now," he said haltingly, "I'm one all right, and I'm very, very thirsty. Please take me to some water right now!"

Later that night, trundling off to bed, Gertie said if, God forbid, the fetus she was carrying came into the world blindsided like Earl, she'd pray as never before that Eddie and she would have the fortitude to do as well as Louisa and the Sutts had by

Earl. Eddie slid beside her till his head rested against her belly, which was finally beginning to show, and swore he heard a gurgle.

Memoir Stories

Tornado Alley

AFTER midnight, even in April, it can get pretty cold around here, especially in the excuse for a station we were waiting in on the other side of Elyria. It's just a shack now, unheated, stuck so close to the tracks it's a wonder trains don't knock it down whizzing past. The phone's torn off the wall; schedules littering the floor are hopelessly out of date; an old magazine's been stripped to its last recipes. We were waiting for the Maestro, as we'd been coached to call him, on the express from Boston.

"Beats me why they even bother to keep this joint open at all, just invites more vandalism," Sheldon said. "We could wait in the van, you know."

Fritz was flapping his arms. "Just think, you guys, the train's only an hour or so late tonight."

I'd been reading a book about amnesiacs. "Do you know the story behind Sherwood Anderson?" I said, to keep my mind off my frozen toes. "He used to run a paint factory right here in Elyria before turning to writing. Seems he got up from his desk one day, walked out, and kept walking. Anyway, there's a photo of the headline from the *Chronicle-Telegram* when he died: 'Paint Manufacturer Passes Away.' I kid you not!"

"Very funny," Sheldon said, taking a quick shot outside with his head. "I'd walk away from Elyria any chance I got. Hey, wait a sec, I think I hear the engine now." We rubbed the cracked window clean and, sure enough, there was the headlight blazing away down the track.

"Hope he's more alive than his picture suggests," Sheldon said. "This is Elyria, remember? We've just got two minutes to whisk him off the train. I hear he travels with more trunks than Elizabeth Taylor."

"One's just for batons, I bet," Fritz said. "Once saw him break a bunch in a TV show, a concert somewhere in Hungary. At first he seemed willing to indulge the bassoonists, but when they really blew it, he hopped down off the box and stuck his stick right in their beefy faces."

"I've heard, on these college junkets," I chipped in, "that he's liable to do most anything—dress down faculty, holler at lazy students, even request traps for the mice under the concert stage."

"God knows we can always use help with students. They pay more attention to an outsider," Sheldon muttered.

The Maestro had been engaged for a month-long residency. For starters, to work with the student orchestra and in our case with the choir as well, because the trustees had found the bucks to commission a new choral work from him. Teaching German, I was asked to stand by in case he'd use any German texts he liked to patch into his other choral compositions, the translation of which I was to supervise if not actually produce myself for the program. I was also to serve as a language coach if students needed help mastering pronunciations. A perfectionist of the first order, the Maestro was known to blow up—and in one case he simply left altogether!—over the slightest flaws vis-à-vis the preparatory work he expected to have been put in. His fee was rumored to be so out of line with what the college normally paid that we were told it was one of the reasons the Dean announced a freeze on salaries at the last faculty meeting—at which Fritz had leaned over to whisper, "For this I left a pretty decent job in Pittsburgh?"

The three of us could have cared less about the hullabaloo over the premiere, especially the pitch about open rehearsals, at which the Maestro agreed to "suffer"—his word—a few questions. The Dean had droned on, "The general public will have the rare opportunity to witness one of the great composers of our time doing what he does best — teaching young musicians at the beginning of what one hopes is a promising career, preparing them for a life of commitment and dedication to the most inclusive art of all." When he finally sat down, Sheldon tapped me on the shoulder, opened his mouth, and stuck a finger down.

What had Sheldon and Fritz more than mildly concerned, not to say downright worried, was the Dean called them in, giving them to understand that the Maestro would be prepared, gratis in fact, to help evaluate their work at this critical juncture of their conservatory careers, inasmuch as they were coming up for tenure soon. Of course, he'd said condescendingly, they had the right to forego "this rare opportunity." On the other hand, blah blah blah, he couldn't imagine any serious musician not welcoming such a review, to see where one stood on the larger landscape the Maestro dominated. Neither Sheldon nor Fritz had the guts to refuse. "A hired gun to pick us off," Sheldon grumbled later over beers.

"Can you imagine him giving a shit about us, off in Bellagio, wined and dined by the Rockefellers?" Fritz said at the P.O., as we stood in line to mail his and Sheldon's identical packages to the Maestro — CVs; tapes; a few, very few, new compositions (who had the time to compose with their load? they'd grumble). And of course, the inevitable student evaluations.

The train barely stopped rolling as a tiny figure dropped out of the door, almost tumbling down the steps like a bat, somehow able to catch the last step; no conductor in sight. "That can't be him," Sheldon said at first.

As if having overheard him, the Maestro called out weakly, "It's me, boys, where in hell are we?" We took hold of his arms and legs and swung him down, trying quick introductions over the noise of the train picking up speed again, till the Maestro waved us off. Later, he seemed to say, so we guided him down the rickety steps leading from the platform to the parking lot where we'd left the van running with the heat on. Suddenly, Fritz realized we were going off without any baggage, but the Maestro said, half-asleep, "Everything I require besides body and what little soul I may claim to will arrive tomorrow by truck, pray God anyway. Lately, I like to travel with minimum fuss." Then he began singing, "Me and my shadow."

"You know this little tune?" He hummed the rest and finished it off with a nimble jig. We looked at one another, clapped and bowed. He seemed quite touched. "My papa used to say, 'No such life for you, sonny boy. Just eat your soupie, be glad we have what we have.' So I gave up a sing and dance career right then and there, in the motherland," the Maestro continued, on a note of genuine disappointment. Then he started coughing, drawing his silk scarf tight around his neck. "We great tenors must take every precaution," he winked as he hopped into the van.

On the way back to the college, all I could focus on was did I have a spare toothbrush somewhere? Wouldn't that be the bare minimum of hospitality? Or perhaps the Maestro had false teeth, just rinsed them out? I turned around to check. "I love American ice cream," he was saying to Fritz, his head almost on Fritz's shoulder. "Much better than the Italian ices I am used to," he went on, as if it were the most natural thing to be discussing at that hour. "Maybe there is open one of your convenience stores. A beautiful invention, yes? Where we could look for some butter pecan, boys?" He said "boys" as we were in his mob, deeply in cahoots. "Ice cream induces sleep, you know. This is a fact, confirmed by my good friend, Professor Hrncire. Maybe you are familiar with his scientific contributions? We joke sometimes we will win the Nobel Prize the same year. Of course, first they must invent one for music. Can you understand why there is none so far yet? Well, never to mind. This is idle chatter. I try Valium sometimes, but ice cream is more fun, yes?" His head sank to his chest and out he went, just like that.

We rolled into town, right through the main stoplight. Nick, the night cop, was slouched down in his cruiser, fast asleep. "Remember the traffic report some students used to do on the college radio station—Midnight on Main Street"? Sheldon said. "Best damn program on the air, complete with the milk truck's squeaking wheels. I couldn't have composed a better score."

Suddenly, the Maestro was with us again, wide awake, one of those brief naps geniuses take, no doubt. He pointed to the Apollo's marquee. "The mouse man," he squealed. "For unknown reasons I love Disney. Maybe they even ask me before I die to do a little music for one of their pictures. I will not say 'no'!"

At the Maestro's dorm quarters, Sheldon volunteered to show him the guest suite, the best the college could offer, but right over the Asia House's stinking kitchen.

"Just keep going, guys. I can walk to my place from here," Sheldon said, so Fritz and I peeled off. The Maestro gave a little wave, like a baby. I drove Fritz out to the farmhouse three miles south of town, where he lived with his wife and son while they looked for a house to buy if tenure came through. We were too wiped out to keep talking. Fritz did mumble something about our brief holiday, come to think: the next day or two, some students on the welcoming committee would be escorting the Maestro around, pointing him in the right direction at the right time, let's hope. But it was 3:00 AM, Sunday morning already, and after I stashed the van in the college garage I headed home, practically sleepwalking.

Sometime in the late afternoon, managing to throw the covers off and breathe again, I set out for the store; milk for the cat and coffee for me. A student was in an aisle with the Maestro in tow, looking over the ice cream assortment. To stay incognito if possible, I waved her off when she motioned me over. The

Maestro had obviously not recognized me, even with his terrifying glasses. I was relieved. They proceeded to the check-out line and I heard him ask her, "My dear, have we eaten lunch yet?" A little dementia can't hurt anyone, I thought.

The first week of the residency seemed to go well, and Sheldon and I even got some tennis in. The new women's coach was annoyed about how much court-time faculty could lay claim to, and she soon started getting her way. Angered, Sheldon would drive us right over the lawns to the courts. "We're playing no matter what. Who's more important, anyway?" he'd yodel. Security was there in force, however, waiting for us behind the net when we tried to squeeze in one last match before course work would consume us. We'd gotten away with playing on our "nickel," Sheldon put it. He'd rip up notes threatening to deduct fines from our paycheck and send them to the coach.

When Sheldon lost a point, a shot he felt he could have otherwise made in his sleep, he'd crack his racquet over the post and toss it over the fence. His back seat was always jammed with spares. His family had so much money he'd think nothing of firing off telegrams from the local Western Union office to all points and people in the land. Sometimes I'd go along to help draft the texts, because he valued my "storehouse of logic and grammar," he'd say somewhat unctuously. Lately, he'd been visibly upset with President Johnson for holding his dogs up by their ears, and even more for showing his belly scar off to reporters. While he was at it, Sheldon shot off telegrams at other Washington targets. Today, on the way back, we hit the state liquor store in Elyria, because Oberlin kept voting itself dry in every election.

"Hey," Sheldon said when we turned into my street, handing me the brandy from the bag under his seat, "there's still half an hour left till the Maestro's open rehearsal session. Let's drop by. Fritz is probably there already, trying to save us seats, too. It was not a bad idea to know what the Maestro said in public, I agreed; especially since Fritz and Sheldon had just received instructions for their one-on-one conferences with the Maestro about their work and had been assigned a time at his studio above the conservatory library.

The chapel's auditorium was so stuffed we were lucky to snake our way up to the balcony. We couldn't see Fritz anywhere in the throng; and besides, he probably had to release the seats he tried to hold for us. So while I wedged in against the back wall, Sheldon persuaded a student he knew to sit on her boyfriend's lap so he could squeeze into their pew. Up above, all the transoms were wide open. Even the pigeons on the roof seemed curious. Below, the aisles were clogged with wires leading every which way to various amplifiers, broadcasting ports, and a TV unit from a Cleveland station perched on a corner platform. All eyes were on the Maestro sitting at the grand piano, ringed by students allowed to join him on stage. A match would have ignited us all.

In the sudden silence of the moment, I felt the Maestro had probably just played a phrase to illustrate a point. After a few last questions — "Why did you choose B-flat minor for the Estonian Mass?" — "Because I never liked this key and wanted to find out why!" — "Who was the greatest influence on you when you were our age?" — "My three girlfriends" (which almost brought down the house) — "What was it like growing up in your homeland?" — "You do not want to know this!" — the moderator signaled for one final question.

One of those kids who probably shouldn't have been wasting his parents' money reached for the mic in the aisle and shouted, "Maestro, have you ever done drugs, man?" The whole place went still, quieter than it had likely ever been.

The Maestro walked slowly to the lip of the stage, just as slowly pushing his glasses up his nose onto his forehead. Then he drew his hands to his hips, leaned out over the first row and said, in his inimitable accent, "With a mind like mine, boys and girls, you don't need drugs!" Before the applause subsided, Sheldon and I hit the stairs. Back at the excuse for a faculty lounge, Fritz finally straggled by; and we agreed that with that performance the college had gotten its money's worth, and then some. Sheldon and he were even looking forward to their conference with the Maestro, now. Well, sort of.

Coming up on Easter, the first of three concerts of the Maestro's choral work was scheduled. The second would close the semester, the third launch graduation ceremonies. So it didn't surprise Sheldon and Fritz, they said later, that the Maestro was quite late for their chats. He apologized profusely but didn't seem to know who Fritz was at all, or why he was there. Sheldon reported something of a similar nature, as he'd had his meeting a day before. "It was weird, man. I can't begin to recount exactly what he said." When I asked how he felt it had gone, Sheldon just shrugged.

Fritz was so rattled he blurted out, "I believe you're supposed to have evaluated my work here so far, sir. Help me get a sense of where I need to go, next; what to work harder on and all. By the way," he continued on a hunch, "I trust my materials reached you in Bellagio?" It dawned on him that might explain why the Maestro didn't seem to know what the hell was up. "I'm coming up for tenure," Fritz went on, "as the Dean must have mentioned, sir …" His voice sank.

"Explain me what is this tenure, please? These things mean different things in different places. That makes my old head swim," he said, so Fritz tried to. The Maestro kept looking at his watch or down at his red shoes. One was untied, and Fritz resisted the urge to tie it. Finally, the Maestro said, "Well, my good fellow, you must go on doing the work of the world. This is my best advice. It is hard work, this life. Yes? And we need the next generation to take its turn. People like you adding their notes to the human symphony." With that he grabbed Fritz's hand and shook it till Fritz gently pulled it away.

On the Tuesday before Palm Sunday, Fritz, Sheldon, and I joined to take stock. They realized the Music Department wasn't about to keep both of them on and flipped a coin to predict which of them would not receive tenure. Fritz won the toss so the drinks were on him. "Let's tap my keg of Iron City at the farmhouse," he said. "Meet you in the parking lot after the last senior recital." I tagged along because some of my German students gave lieder recitals. We were just about through all the obligatory recitals at semester's end.

We were settling into some serious drinking—Fritz already having opened a second keg while his wife shushed the baby in the bedroom off the kitchen—when I blurted out, "Okay, here's the deal, guys. When they offer tenure just to Fritz, we all flat out resign, give every student an A, and pull up stakes." Their friendship was so important to me I was quite willing to look for another job, too, not exactly sure I really wanted a career teaching German. Fairly foot-loose, I wanted to assure them of solidarity for us all. Then I started gagging, Fritz banged me on the back, and Sheldon pumped his thumbs, tipping his chair way back.

Fritz closed his eyes. "All well and good for you loners to lark it up, especially with your moola, Sheldon, but some of us like a regular meal now and then, not to mention Pampers and Pablum for my parents' only grandson."

"When he wakes up," Sheldon whimpered, "tell him my folks have threatened to adopt a grandkid if I don't produce one soon."

I reached over to grab Fritz's arm. "Blood pressure's slightly elevated, but he'll recover."

Fritz brushed me off. "Know what? Just to be rid of you two the college would send you off with a parade."

"Too many brews have turned him sour," Sheldon whispered.

I tipped my head toward the bedroom door. The baby had started crying. Fritz's wife said something through the door, and Fritz finally pushed off to join them.

"So long, then, been good to know you," Sheldon and I duoed.

When the sirens went off all over town early on Palm Sunday morning, I thought at first the state police were finally moving in on a drug bust we knew was in the works. The college had been winking at a bunch of students known to be hard users. But when the wind really kicked up, so fierce it sent the old maple next to my cottage down on the garage, I ran to the window. The lightning was tremendous. The sky turned milky green, so eerie my pulse raced. Wires started snapping, whipping through the air. A lone car stopped mid-street and two souls jumped out, fleeing for who knows where. Good thing, too, because a giant elm came crashing down just short of their car. If I'd known about tornadoes back then, I'd have made for the cellar, or at least dived under a table, found a closet to crawl into. What I did instead was go back to bed, blithely assuming it'd all blow over eventually, and buried my head in the pillow till I blotted out the noise and somehow got back to sleep, if fitfully. Sheldon woke me around noon, furiously knocking away at the door.

"My God, man, haven't you heard the news?" he yelled upstairs. "A tornado's hit just south of town. Come on, we've got to check on Fritz and family. They say the church at the crossroads near their farmhouse is completely gone. We can't get through by car, but maybe our bikes can make it." When I looked down he was shaking all over. "Step on it, man," he yelled.

"Give me a sec," I yelled back. Luckily, the tree down on the garage hadn't blocked off my bike. On the way around the streets we couldn't negotiate, we ran into one of his con students out scouting the damage.

"Haven't you heard," she screamed across the street, "everything's been canceled, classes and everything!"

"The concert, too?" Sheldon shouted.

"Jeez, man, it's a fucking disaster out here, you blind or something?"

By the time we made it out to Fritz's, rescue crews were already on the scene, with dogs sniffing away under wreckage strewn across the entire landscape, it seemed. Fritz and his son had been found dead, a fireman said quietly, but the Mrs. was safe at the hospital in Elyria. "We found her under a bookcase." He kept shaking his head, his hands still trembling. We just stood there, the three of us, unable to move, letting the tears come. Finally, the fireman said, "Well, better get back to town myself, file my report. Can I give you guys as lift?" We waved him off gently and just stared at what was left of the farmhouse. It seemed no higher than an inch.

Sheldon kept shuffling around in a circle. I took a deep breath and tried to hold it. When he got his legs moving again, he made for the back fields. I saw him motion furiously and forced myself to his side. Near the barn, where Fritz had planned to keep a horse so their son could learn to ride, the fridge leaned heavily to one side, its door ajar. All we could see inside was a single lemon, which I took.

When we got to the chapel for the services the following week, Sheldon and I headed for a side pew separate from the rest of the music faculty. The college chaplain placed his arm lightly around Fritz's wife, who was heavily bandaged, and led her and various family members down to the front pew. Then he and the dean moved to the podium.

I was about to busy myself with the program when Sheldon

whispered, "Don't look now but the Maestro's coming down our aisle." When he reached our row, he looked over, faltering a moment, then steadied himself with a hand to the pew. Behind his thick lenses, his eyes seemed to be blinking nonstop. Then he continued on to the small organ in the corner. Everyone was at great pains not to stare in his direction. Our surprise broke when he started to play Bach's little piece, *Alle Menschen müssen sterben*. I don't recall anything else.

"Well, guess we'd better get in line at the reception, pay our respects, don't you think?" Sheldon said. I nodded and we signed the guestbook at the back before joining the crowd in the meeting room. We made our way along the family but when we got to Fritz's wife I froze. Sheldon had to rescue me. "You and Fritz and your dear little boy will always be in our prayers," he managed to say, nudging me along toward the refreshments after she patted our cheeks. After piling my plate high, thinking I could eat my way past sorrow, I caught sight of the Maestro standing at a window behind the buffet.

"I know who you are," he began when we ventured near. "You are the nice boys who picked me up and took good care of me that first night. I am very, very sorry about your colleague."

He held out both hands and we each took one, standing there a moment mindlessly sipping our punch. Finally, spurred by the moment, I just blurted out, "How about joining us for a real drink, Maestro. Are you free to leave now?" He too seemed eager to slip away.

We took our time getting to Jamie's Bowling Bar outside town, a hangout for escaping from academia into a swirl of smoke, beer and bluster guaranteed to reset the most dulled among us. The Maestro took our arms as we ushered him to a dark booth near the alleys. It wasn't much of an enterprise: three lanes, which were starting to light up for the night's trade. Quaffing the foam off "please, the darkest beer you can tap," the Maestro said, pointing to the rack of bowling balls, "I would like to try this sport sometime. When I was in knickers only the common folk went bowling. Not quite your sport but a little like it, except the pins were just set up anywhere outside, and the ball is much smaller. When my best friend's father died, they buried him with his lucky ball. He was the champion bowler of the whole area."

After knocking back a few more brews, we rented some shoes and scouted for balls. I kept holding balls out with two holes for the Maestro to poke his fingers into, but he shook his head and pointed to one with three. Sliding his thumb and elegant fingers into the holes, he cradled the ball to his chest like a baby. After we gave him a few quick pointers, he righted his body and made for the line with tiny steps. The ball seemed to come off his hand on its own, and he nearly fell down. Promptly finding the gutter, the ball skittered on down the lane and he grinned. "How is your expression—practice, practice makes perfect?"

Right after the graduation concert, he left by private limo. We never heard from him again. Sheldon was let go, of course, and I suspect Fritz wouldn't have been tenured either. Every so often, Sheldon sends me a holiday card; reports he's still hacking away, teaching more in uglier places, composing less, "no great shakes" he always ends on. Except, as Fritz would say, we're off the streets, paying the bills. Got your card, I'll write to Sheldon, but still no word from Fritz.

Some Lunkers

WE live in a small town tucked away in a corner of the county. If you jump in your car, you're at a cornfield in a few minutes. The call to go fishing here is quite strong; small ponds nearby boast of strapping bass and chunky bluegills. Old Woman's Creek, only an hour distant, is a healthy flowage with plenty of challenges from the moment you set your boat in till you reach Lake Erie, where the creek mouths a few miles north.

But nine times out of ten we head for Spencer Lake. Twenty-two miles to the south, it's ringed by dark farms and thick woods. When you're out on the water it's as if you're way up north, fishing Wisconsin lakes we knew as a child. I say "we" because we generally fish in twos and threes, though actually it's really every man for himself. It's a chance to be alone, in a setting where thoughts come and grow without the worry of anyone intruding before the mind knows where it wants to dwell, though there is kind of a comradery we all seek; a chance to get off with someone you like, someone you work with, but perhaps don't know too well. Like fathers and sons who wait for summer vacations to talk more intimately, decant feelings bottled in the usual course of things.

It's Saturday when we back the car up to the garage where the boat sits. David and I each take a handle and push it up on the trunk. He looks over nervously as it scrapes along before it catches on the top bar of the carrier and drops into place. "The hell with scratches, David, that's what this '65's for," I say—but there is something to a feeling bred into us about damaging a car's finish, never mind the Ford's ready for fifty-cent sledgehammer hits at the local benefits.

Our hearts have jumped out to the lake already. We're driving off feeling euphoric about having kept our gear in shape over the long winter. The sweetest job, the one my dad made the most of, was taking the reel completely apart and oiling it to perfection before slipping it back into the little leather pouch. Turning the corner, we suddenly remember the oars we've left behind! The oars my wife and I couldn't bear to store in the garage when we bought the boat. They were so beautiful we marched them up into the bedroom, leaning them in the corner like Norse artifacts. More than once we'd had to use branches for oars at the lake. We pull up back up the drive sheepishly.

"Bob's might be open this early, David. Let's try to pick up some minnows from him." We head right over to his "Bait Barn" at the edge of town before angling down south on 301 to Spencer Lake Road. Bob waves from his mower as we drive up. He always looks dressed for fishing but hasn't gone in years; says it's the "arthuritis." His mutt, tied to a stake in the yard, starts yelping so he takes a moment to talk her down. He's the genuine article, as are all those pictures of him and his old buddies tacked on the wall, stringers of salmon, trout, pike, and bass streaming from their hands. He's got the stories to back them up, too. We've been tantalized by bits and snatches over the years, but he's not one to waste talk; and in the exchange of information, mostly his, on water and weather conditions, he seems to be sizing us up. We're careful to answer him directly, never exaggerate the size of a catch when he asks. We joke that if we took him to the diner for his favorite rhubarb pie, he'd maybe start in on a few of his secrets—but of course he'd never tell even his best buddy exactly where he sank his old Model T at Parson's Reservoir one super cold winter—just drove it out on the ice and a sudden thaw sent it down somewhere before anyone got a fix on the spot. "Best damn crib this side of the Ozarks," is all he'd ever say. All of

SOME LUNKERS

us would-be fisher-folk around town agree on one thing: we've never caught as much as Bob thought we should on any given day.

"These minnies ain't the best, so I won't charge you the usual. The damn truck I get 'em by from Mansfield lost its coolant, something like that," he says, throwing in a few extra for good measure. We just nod and he heads back to the mower, quieting his mutt on the way. The poor quality of the minnows keeps us checking on them as we putt along, when we ought to be leaning into the morning, amping up our spirits for a few pure hours away from it all. There's some choice about which back roads to take into the lake, but we're eager to get there and settle for the fastest way. Though we've driven the route many times, I overshoot the turnoff; so we wind up going through Spencer itself, something of a speed trap, but Chief Hendrick waves us on through, unaccountably! Actually, the detour quiets us down, and we even stop to inspect a tree we'd always wondered about. Turns out it's an Osage orange, so we help ourselves to a few of the ball-like fruits for setting by the doors to our houses. The faint odor they give off is said to keep insects from crawling in.

The first thing we notice turning down the access road to the lake is it's as rough as ever. The mud holes haven't shifted an inch, but at least there are no new ones; and there's a brand new ramp down to the water, the asphalt's creamy black pulling us right down to the ripples on the sand. We slide the boat off in record time, blow on our hands and feast on sun and mist rising together. It's still a bit chilly as we shove off. David points to a lazy heron circling the crown of its nest in a tree across the bay. For a moment we feel transported to some foreign landscape before the movie's begun. It shouldn't matter if we manage to catch anything.

Spencer is actually two small lakes split by a causeway with a large culvert connecting both halves. Fishermen and fishes can pass back and forth easily between them. You just hunch down in your boat and pull yourself along by the ridges in the culvert's corrugated metal siding. People stroll the causeway, picnic on the greensward dropping down to the water, fish from its gently sloping banks. Fish prefer structure like rocks, walls, and dams, causeway country in short, so we'd do better to start fishing there. But having grown up fishing the piers along Lake Michigan, I want to get away from the pier gang. Spencer's so tiny in the surround you can't get away from the causeway for more than a few hundred yards, but like mirrors in a small room, its two halves make it seem larger. Besides, we're the first ones out in a boat, have our pick of spots. David sticks an oar in the water to push us off the sandbar running the length of the shore. Just past the reeds the boat rocks free and we're off.

We haven't been out for more than half an hour, following the deeper channel between the north shore and the culvert through the causeway, when David makes out something off our bow. I row over to where he points, and we see quite a commotion in the brackish water. Swinging the boat around so we can both look from the same side, we're dumbfounded: right on the surface, as if in some sort of trance, responding to a strange call or worse, perhaps some kind of virus, is a sizeable chain pickerel. It thrashes about, seems to be chasing its tail, suddenly reverses direction, flops over, and goes quiet for a moment before repeating the ritual.

We watch it spellbound. Finally, David says, "Do you suppose we should net it, see what's wrong? Is that against some law?" None I know of, so he dips the net under the fish and boats it. As if in shock, it lies there motionless for a moment. We make out some gashes in its side, figure something bigger must have gone after it. Hunching over, we're just about to pare away the netting when it strikes—the kind of leap designed to cut your hand open! We pull back in the nick of time. I don't need another hint and firmly hook its jaw with a finger. The fish goes entirely numb; we snap it on the stringer and get it overboard, whereupon it straightens out at once, behaving like any catch. Nothing seems wrong with it at all!

Lucky as we feel about plucking it from the water like that, we can't let well enough alone. David says, "Well, that's our first one, now let's get some more to keep it company." We agree not to mention how we "caught" this one.

I hold the pickerel up one more time, measuring it with my eye. It's fully twenty-five inches, must be about five pounds. I fool some more, "David, what did you say you caught this on? Bait companies like to know if they're involved." We're so happy we guzzle an early beer, drinking to even bigger fish.

I could begin to lie now, try to get you to believe we had a marvelous time of it, that that was only the beginning of a fabulous outing, even throw in some fake description, put otters and muskrats in the picture, dwell on rare birds swooping past, the whole bit. But the truth is, the pickerel spooked us. Our brains went from pink to gray; we lost all energy. We fished all right, went through all the usual motions in just the right spots till late afternoon. We also held up the poor pickerel at regular intervals, shook our heads, grinned a lot. We even talked more than usual about our jobs, our kids, our lives. But we didn't so much as feel anything on our rods except the dragonflies, losing ourselves in the intricacies of their shiny blue wings. Till sundown. When the other thing happened. The thing rounding this all out that will forever keep the story alive, right down to our rocking-chair days on the nursing home porch.

We'd drifted all over the north half of the lake, at one point considering pushing through the causeway to the southern half, where it's said the really big ones lurk. We did squint back toward the culvert entrance when it clouded over. It's a sweet place to sit a storm out, taking in what might be blowing by from the tunnel of a nest. But once you choose the north half, the southern one seems very far off, as if in another country, another way of life. (Maybe you don't go through to the other side because the mirror works only if you don't walk into it?) So there we were, tied up to one end of an old log peeled white by sun and water, still-fishing in the deepest part of the lake. When it happened.

Five o'clock on the dot. We'd agreed to leave. The night fishermen were beginning to arrive. A guy we'd seen before, who fished the shore in waders and generally landed some lunkers, was ambling along the path to the rock he always cleaned his pipe on. We saw him light up and waved. We stowed the rods first. When they were cleared, I pulled up my pole—in Ohio you're allowed two poles of any kind; we usually used casting rods but flung a pole out to the side—and released my minnow. It had enough life left to nose down into deeper water, which always makes you happy. I remember David twisting his pole up in the anchor rope. When he worked it free and stood up to raise his bait, he shouted, "My God, it's alive!" Which tuned me like a fork. He lurched a bit, sat back down with his hand guiding the way, then he raised the pole straight up over his head and lifted, and kept lifting. Instinctively, I reached for the net and nearly fell to his side. It seemed he was pulling up something as heavy as a safe. It came straight up and as I leaned over the side I could see a head. Massive, like a St. Bernard's. David pulled it up over the rim of the net and let it settle down into the webbing. Then we hauled it in together, David pulling on the line with his hands while I worked the net handle. It took us a moment to realize it was just a crappie. A white crappie, I noticed. A panfish, it's only a panfish, I remember thinking. My God, it's only a panfish, which I kept repeating to myself. We didn't say anything till we eased it off the hook and onto the stringer with the pickerel.

We both knew we'd better not admire it out of the water too long. Crappies are extremely delicate: one flop and they'll disintegrate before your eyes if you don't get them some water pronto. Before the notion it could be a record fish really set in, we slipped it back into the water and just sat there a while, not even bothering to swat the dusk's first mosquitoes. "But David," I finally blurted out, "this could be a record! Do you know what happens when you catch a record fish, *any* kind of fish? Trucks roll up to your door, trucks full of prizes, pleasure boats, sports clothes, motors, oil for a year, line for a lifetime!"

At bottom, it was a freak of a fish. Truly a monster crappie. But *how* big? We couldn't tell; we had nothing along to measure it except a bitty scale and a ruler that slides out to twelve inches. My son's, we'd nudge it into my tackle box for trips to the town reservoir. Then I remembered the ranger station at the entrance to the lake. Possibly there was someone still on duty, so we made like crazies, rowed the top off the water, dragging the fish out of the water every so often so they wouldn't drown in our wake. I remembered all those record-breaking fish displayed in ice-chests outside sporting goods stores from my fishing days back in Wisconsin. The fish had to be brought right in, measured and weighed, or else dehydration would set in and shrink them away, so any chance of a record would disappear.

We hit shore and kept running. The boat could have drifted back out to the middle of the lake, and we wouldn't have noticed or cared. Holding the fish up between us, we ran toward the ranger station.

There were two of them, just closing up, one wiping his hands on a rag. He couldn't quite finish "Gentlemen, what can we do for you?" because he caught sight of the crappie. "Jeez," he yelled to his partner, "Where's the damn record book, Mike? I think we've got ourselves something here all right!" While his partner flipped the pages, he laid the crappie out on a yardstick, smoothing it as far as it would stretch, and jotted something down we couldn't see. Then he made his way to a scale on the workbench in the clutter at the back of the shed. He pushed the center-weight over, the crappie lay still for the ceremony, and it was all over in a second. "Nope, sorry, you guys just missed it by a bit. Real sorry about that. Would have been great for all of us, you know."

That jerked us out of our excited gaze. "Hey, how long is it anyway, what's it weigh?" David said. The ranger handed us the little slip with the numbers: 19 ¼"; 3 lbs. 1 oz. David folded it up to stick in his wallet. The rangers gave us some newspaper to wrap it in and noticed the pickerel.

"Quite a day you had yourselves out there," Mike said, grinning. We should have been happy, but I think we weren't. I think we're still not happy. We took our time getting home.

A second wave of excitement did wash over us as we pulled into town. At least we could finally show some lunkers to our wives and kids, who'd been all too kind the days we were skunked, or caught just a little something for our troubles. First of course we had to drive around the town square for some swaggering. At the drugstore Art looked up from the prescription counter and just whistled. Then on to George's barbershop. He was the best damn fisherman in these parts, and we wanted to make him drool.

George nearly dropped his shears when we held the fish up to his window. "Hey, where'd you dudes get those, *that* sucker there?" he said, waving us in. Sniffing the crappie, he muttered, "Be damned, maybe I'll do me some fishing again one of these days." He'd given up going out lately, and had settled for a huge fish tank in his shop, complete with baby sharks. He'd even taken to selling tropical fish on the side. But his eye was on a record now, we could tell. "Hey you guys," he yelled after us as we headed for the door, "you be careful fixing that crappie, it doesn't want much cooking." We slid back into the car and drove out to David's.

His kids ran for the camera, and after David took a roll of pictures we cleaned the fish and slapped them on their sink for supper. The next morning, at the office, David said they cooked the crappie too long, turned it to mush. But the pickerel, in spite of all its bones, that strong gamey odor, the fish almost no one bothers with, was wonderful.

Czechoslovakia

THE visa application makes no bones. "Purpose of Trip— Person(s) You Intend To Visit," so I start worrying long before I leave: should I lie or tell the truth? I compromise, block in TO STUDY CZECH POETRY WITH PROF. DR. KAREL SOUKUP. Not the writer's real name, for reasons that are obvious. It worked on a trip to East Germany, all those titles; I even tacked on DIREKTOR for special occasions, made someone bow a little lower. As for studying Czech poetry, well, there must be a lot, but I'm really only interested in Soukup's. He hadn't published a book for years. The visa comes back so fast from Chicago I almost don't notice it's just for seven days. I'd planned on thirty. At the local travel bureau I settle on the cheapest way: charter to Munich, train the rest.

Landing in Munich, I make for the station. The train's late, so there's time for a telegram to Soukup in Prague. With luck, he'll get it in time to meet me. I write it using all the abbreviations I can think of. Are words really worth that much? The clerk's unbearably rude to a Turkish worker ahead of me trying to wire money home. I want to say something fierce but quickly drop my outrage: who needs trouble now? At the Information Center I bargain for a room near the station. The desk clerk's reading Grass's latest novel and lets me have the shower key free. I wake up singing silly German folksongs about meadow flowers named Erika, but know deeper down German soldiers sang these ditties in the teeth of the worst battles. The train's at the border before I know it.

We're switched to a side track. The little schedule on the

window ledge (*Nicht Hinauslehnen!*) says expect the border check to take two hours. I open the window for a glimpse of Czech fields and am so startled I cry out: two pathetically young soldiers in ragged uniforms that seem cut from old carpets point their Tommy guns up at me. One has his boot on the rail, scratches his crotch. The other's walking a mean and mangy German shepherd slowly along the track, searching the undercarriage. Why would anyone want to sneak *into* Czechoslovakia? Dragging the window up, I can see that all the way down the line there are guards, two to a car, odd twins. I try the window on the station side. Some old men, dressed like generals in an operetta with rouge on their faces, are marching along in the shape of a jail cell. Inside is what appears to be an American who's jumping up and down, gesturing wildly, yelling: "Why in hell did you break my camera? You didn't have to do that! Jesus Christ, I've got a valid passport from your own embassy in Washington, that's in America! I'm supposed to cover the trials. Jesus!" I hear someone trudging down the aisle and edge back into my compartment.

It's a man, with a woman right behind him. In the same cheap uniforms everyone else is wearing. He asks me in garlicky German, "Have you camera?" I shake my head. He reaches for my briefcase on the seat and easily finds the nails a student gave me, a sheet full of them taped down with little captions beneath like haikus. It's for Soukup, who's building a house in the suburbs of Prague. If he'd use what she called magical nails, it would never fall apart, she told me to tell him. My favorite's the delicate Queen's Nail, with a little collar-like projection right under the head. "*Wozu das?*" The guard pokes each nail with his thumb.

I break into slangy German. "Harmless, pal. Just a harmless little gift for a friend. Can't hurt a flea, honest." He turns the page over, holding it up to the dim bulb in the ceiling. I start blabbing something about how many cartons of cigarettes I have in my suitcase, but he motions the woman in and backs out saluting.

She's severely beautiful, a veritable Hedy Lamarr, and flips open a case like the ones cigarette girls carry in clubs. It's chock full of money! I exchange just the minimum required, figuring I'll do better in a big bank: a dumb move that will cost me hours in downtown Prague waiting for six official signatures before I hear my number called.

The train starts up slowly and never picks up speed, as if a child turned his transformer to full and the juice ran out. It grows dark in spurts. I can barely make out some farmers in a field sweeping scythes from side to side. There's smoke from roofs that seem without chimneys. The dominant sound is of rushing water. I've read that, unlike other Eastern European countries, Czechoslovakia has all the water it needs. Each stop takes us farther back into the darkness tunneling around us. A peeling sign saying MARIENBAD appears, giving off a faint yellow light. Is that where they made the movie? I look hard for a mansion by the tracks, but just the same old station-set pops up, triggered by the train at every stop. Drawing away from Marienbad, everything out the window now is woods. Dark green at first, then darker and darker green, going to darkest green at the side of your eye; and finally, one long curve opening up to blazing white stags against the trees. I imagine hearing baying hounds, the sound of a musket. The animals slowly fade into the mist. And finally, Prague, coming up out of the darkest darkness, as if that's all there's left.

The main railway station glistens, painfully antiseptic. I'm the only one off my car. The whole train seems to have brought to Prague just a dozen souls, who all disappear before I realize I don't have a coin for a phone call. But there's an attendant at the booth! I try German, English, even some broken Italian, but he waves his hands and hops off like a bird. Fighting to calm down, I consider pulling what seems be a fire alarm; but exhaustion pushes me against a pillar, and I shut my eyes. When I wake up, he's there: suddenly, in a scarf large enough for two, nodding slightly. We do the You-Must-Be routine, fall into a hug, push each other off like boxers after a clinch. It turns out to be a minor miracle: the telegram I sent was almost not delivered, all those abbreviations appearing to be code. Then, just as oddly, the clerk must have let it pass at the last minute. There it was, sticking out of Soukup's mailbox when he came home from the clinic.

Soukup had never been down to this brand-new station so he wants to stroll around some. He says it's the butt of jokes already because it's been so poorly built. "With cheap Russian materials, and even cheaper Czech labor," Soukup whispers. We look around one last time before heading to his car. The door handle on his side's wired shut, and there's a drunk draped over the hood. Soukup is firm but kind, pulls him off gently, and joins in on the last little bit of song he's chirping. Wishing us well, it turns out, for the New Year! "And a big fat carp for your table, sir," Soukup wishes him, before he points the drunk away from the road. I ask Soukup to sing the Czech verses again and start to tune in, reminded of my Czech gramma singing me to sleep with similar sounds.

We've barely driven a block when I bring up the matter of the trials. The whole world is watching what will happen to the dissident writers facing years in prison, I offer naively. Soukup confirms, yes, the trials are indeed steaming on at this very moment and the tension's mounting. Student groups are getting noisy in the coffee houses, and some workers seem ready to try something. There are even reports of Russian tanks rumbling toward Prague. "How in hell did you manage to get through?" he says. I tell him about the journalist. He says we'll really have to be careful, but laughs. It doesn't matter? It does? We quickly move to another subject. He's happy I'm willing to stay in the rooming house he's found. It's bound to be safer, more relaxed than the official hotels for tourists where one can easily be watched. The renters seemed nice enough when he made the arrangements. They cater mostly to Finnish and Swedish engineers busy changing Czech architecture. We should be able to talk fairly freely there. The streets are so deserted that Soukup decides on an elaborate detour to show me the route he took home that day in '68 to avoid Russian tanks and barricades at the start of the "Prague Spring."

I tell him I've already seen bullet holes in the parliament building some years ago on a tour with American students. He's clearly disappointed, wants this to be my first trip here. We drive round and round little hills on the edge of town looking for the rooming house. The fog's thick now, the temperature's falling. Passersby we stop for directions are short with Soukup, and hurried. It's almost midnight when we eliminate all the buildings but one, and sure enough, there's the landlady's name on a piece of porcelain wired to the fence. We ring and wake everyone up: the engineers in modern Finnish pajamas; a Czech couple, who seem to step out of the deep past. She has a long braid swinging down her back; her husband's wearing a woodsman's jacket over his nightgown. The roomers push back up to sleep after nods and handshakes, and as I'm shown around the flat I try to memorize which set of towels and washcloths hanging in the WC is mine. The flush of the common toilet's so loud I cringe, and whisk back down to Soukup who's dozed off in the car.

We both need a talk this first night, late though it is. So we tool around looking for a restaurant, finally find one with a jagged hole in the front door. The rumor is another Russian-Czech brawl the night before. In fact, all during my visit someone's always adding up the score of these scrapes and pointing out bullying Russians on street corners in their silly fur hats and shabby coats, staring in one direction like penguins huddled over eggs on a glacier. The restaurant's perfect, because the noise is on a level with punk rock. We won't be overheard, but lean in close to be sure. The Moravian wine's thick and surly, exactly the right thing to drink when learning how bad things really are.

A safer subject is Soukup's new baby, how healthy she is, how happy the grandparents are—they come up from the country every chance they have; and how surprised he was to find the name of his favorite American poet on the official babies' names list. Actually, there are two lists. One for Jews, one for Christians. "Talk about what's in a name," Soukup laughs. At first, forgetting they're not Jewish, they wanted Sarah. When they came to their senses, they found Denisa, thanks to the whim, perhaps, of some minor official, whose turn it was to compile the yearly lists. The Soukups have since heard there are perhaps one or two other Denisas in all the land. If and when things ever return to normal, they joke they'll try to get them all together, and invite Denise Levertov to a party "for the ages."

As for the rest of our talk that night, we started in on who was getting published in Czechoslovakia and who wasn't, and why. Then Soukup told the story of the Writer's Union, that slab of a building you can stroll past but no writer enters. Just a maid occasionally wanders around, pretending to dust. And the story of how someone's children's book was stopped in the middle of publication. Turned out the hero, a badger, looked suspiciously like the president. So the writer, looking forward to her first publication in years—a harmless, charming children's story— got the "red letter": "Unfortunately, Comrade, we are not able to proceed with publication at this time ..." Written and signed by a relation of hers who works for the State Publishing House! When the waiter saunters over to collect, I try to learn the word for "thank you" (*Dekuji*), but have to settle for "you're welcome" (*Prosim*). So beautiful, such an easy word to say compared to *Dekuji* that I use it all the time, asking questions, favors, forgetting what I'm actually saying. No one laughs. People just say it back.

The next morning I'm to report to the police station in my

district. Within the first twenty-four hours of your stay, you must report in, sign multiple forms, pay your respects, make clear you're not about to become a burden to the State. The station must have been a bomb shelter during the war. Everything is heavily padded, the heaviest padding of all on doors bulging out into the corridor. There's a long line of people too well-dressed to be Czechs, waiting to be called. Some smoke nervously, others walk around in tight circles. One woman's reading a Dickens' novel partly aloud. I bite my tongue to keep from asking her which one. It's clear we are not to knock on a door that opens from time to time, a hand in a sleeve waving the next person in line in. Two hours creep by, nothing moves. Then the outside doors blow open, and a raving Italian's being escorted physically down our ranks and through another door at the far end of the hall. He's yelling something about an accident not being his fault, my limited Italian figures out. His Borsalino is knocked from his head, but no one picks it up. Then it's my turn. I'm both frightened and angry when I enter the inner chambers. I approach one of six desks gingerly, but a clerk motions me stiffly to another, who motions me to a third. I stand as still as possible for several minutes before the boy looks up from writing something. He seems a close relative of the boys who searched our train, as rude with words as they were with their guns. I repeat I shall be sure to spend the minimum ten dollars a day. He doesn't care about anything else, my date of birth, where I'm from, just keeps insisting, "ten dollars, ten dollars. You must spend at least ten American dollars every day in our country; and you keep receipts, show them at the border or you no leave. Otherwise we not let you out, understand?" He presses the rubber stamp down hard, but his initials leave almost no trace on my visa.

That evening Soukup takes me to the *Zlata Studna* (Golden Well), an elegant pub just off the castle we'd been visiting earlier. After wolfing down a superb stew, with a good local wine to warm us even more, we head back out to snowflakes falling lazily, some moon and stars clouded to their outlines. The buildings of state we walk around are capped by gargoyles we can barely make out. "Do you remember," Soukup breaks the eerie silence, "those are the gargoyles in my poem you've been working on. Sorry to say the angels aboard are nowhere in evidence now. But look at that one leaning out from its perch. Its beak's too tiny to hold a minnow." But they're so covered by soot I don't see what he knows is there, so we break off to find the car, angling down the cobbled street. It's choked with tiny houses, one sporting a plaque claiming Kafka once roomed there. Maybe seeing his name suddenly reminds us we've forgotten Soukup's poems and essays in the pub, so we race back up the street and just make it through the portcullis to the inner circle where the pub is, past the sleepy guard mumbling something about closing time. Soukup takes a moment to tip him, which earns us a toothy smile.

The pub's gone dark so we pound on the door. Recognizing us, our waiter opens up, a pinch of a cigarette in the corner of his mouth. We fear Soukup's papers have been confiscated, and someone may be photocopying them this very instant. The relief of finding them on the sill next to our table gets us breathing normally again. Ambling back through the gate to the town below, we yell *Prosim* to the guard, who points to his watch, pumping his legs up and down. "*Mach schnell*," he grunts, reminding us of the curfew.

The next morning, apropos of nothing, Soukup says, "Let's go shopping. I need to see what my wife's spending our money on now. Besides, it'll give you another window into this crazy country. We ordered a carpet months ago for the new house, which we may never get. In fact, there may not be a carpet out there at all, but we wouldn't want *them* to know that, would we?" On the way to town, we pass huge apartment complexes rising right up out of mud. They're old enough for people to be living in, but the buildings have not been connected to the street by sidewalks. In fact, sidewalks don't seem to be part of the project at all. We see people changing shoes at the bus stop for the trip to work. Coming home at night, they fish their old dirty shoes from a sack for the trudge back through the mud to their door. It doesn't seem to bother them. "It would," Soukup says, "if they knew sidewalks were a possibility."

"*Koberce*" (carpets) in pale white neon letters hangs from the store like a marquee. The store's owned by the same family that opened it a hundred years ago. We march up three flights of stairs into thin air, it seems, when someone looking like a silent film star escorts Soukup up a fourth flight to a tiny door set into the wall. I drift over to a small group of customers, silent and stiff as mannequins, circling a pile of carpets sitting in the center of showroom. Every so often, someone lifts the top of a carpet with a cane, or someone else squats to peel back the carpets one by one with a gloved hand for others to inspect. Carpet after carpet has a dull pattern of lines crossing lines on a beige or gray background with an occasional circle of red or black setting the whole design off badly. I imagine they're all from Russia, courtesy of Volga Mills, part of a trade for superior Czech ball bearings and vintage Czech chocolate.

When he comes back down from his talk with the top salesman, Soukup is fuming. More unaccountable delays are ahead, he reports with an edge to his voice I've never heard. And inasmuch as a delivery system doesn't exist, he will have to collect their carpet himself or hire someone to haul it out to the suburb where their house is being built, with the same sort of unaccountable delays about most anything. He tries one last dose of sarcasm, but it's lost on a junior clerk showing us to the door. We try to unwind over Turkish coffee and brandy in the corner café. "What else would you like to look into, next?" Soukup says. Besides working on his poems I'm trying to translate, struggling especially to get just the right tone to his brooding wit, I run off three requests: to visit my great gramma's grave in Senica, a four-hours' drive south of Prague—she was murdered by the S.S. at the age of 101, during the last months of WW II, in front of family and neighbors; to visit the seamstress school where her daughter, my gramma, had studied; and to visit Kafka's grave as well.

That afternoon, from his office at the Clinic for Experimental Medicine, where Soukup directs the immunology department, and where he takes me to view the famous Czech nude mice that are bred for cancer research, he calls the appropriate bureau for permission to travel to Senica. He figures things will go more smoothly on his official line, rather than calling from home. When he hears, "It won't be possible, Professor," he can't believe such a harmless request has been denied, but he knows not to ask why. Finally, he says to me, "We must behave as if everything's normal, but keep asking our harmless questions, keep living, keep dying." Our eyes mist up, and he apologizes for thinking how easy it would have been to drive into the countryside, how much I'd have enjoyed the little trip to Senica itself, not to mention how much it means to me to get there. He won't have anything for an excuse, however, not even Russian tanks on manoeuvres, the usual explanation. We both look off through the window at some goats grazing behind the clinic.

As if to distract us further, a lab assistant brings some nude mice over on a tray. They're buried under wood shavings. All I see at first are dozens of beady eyes. The assistant finds a tail, pulls one up, swings it to and fro, and puts it on my arm. Then she coaxes it back down to her palm. I remember my gramma making a mouse from a large handkerchief, popping it along her arm by flexing her muscles. I touch the rubbery skin, which feels like a rhino's I once felt at a zoo. Then it hits: where's the fur? Incredible, something we know by one skin, in another. Something so fetal I look around for a tube to slide it in. The scientist in charge of the current experiment looks in just as we're about to feed the mouse Friskies-like tidbits. "What are you doing, he fairly shouts, "that's unsterile food, you'll ruin our data!"

"But Professor," she says sadly, "what difference does it make? No one cares anymore." Later, she tells us experiments are constantly set back due to a lack of this or that drug, and frequently interrupted for inane bureaucratic reasons. The staff admire the professor for still caring, but lapse into careless ways behind his back. They pet the mice, and by so doing introduce more than enough foreign bodies to vitiate results. "See that computer over there on the landing?" she says. "It's from our Russian benefactors, been there for months. Even the professor can't get anyone to connect it, nor can Dr. Soukup," she says, bowing toward him. He flashes her a fake scowl. All I see is a large bulky shape covered by dirty canvas and tied down with thick rope, the way you'd keep something from sliding on a ship's deck. We break for lunch—cups of luscious Bulgarian yogurt and homemade salami on rye, from the bottom shelf of the little fridge where nude mice blood samples are stored. Such repast in a Czech lab seems quite fitting. On the way out, Soukup suggests we head to the cemetery where Kafka's buried, see if the site's open to the public. On occasion, for unknown reasons—as he likes to say a lot—it's suddenly off-limits. Just to make sure, so we don't waste precious fuel, he stops at a roadside phone to call the Bureau of Cemeteries. Someone answering says it's safe to drive over. To celebrate, we munch away on dessert: Polish apples!

The tiny Jewish Cemetery is backed right up against the enormous Christian one. We park nearby and pick our way along a muddy path to a wrought-iron gate. Expecting it to swing open, we give a push but it pushes back cold. "Karel, is this normal, didn't they tell you it'd be open?"

"Wait," he says, "these buzzers must ring in the caretaker's cottage over there." We push all three for good measure. Nothing. So we try the middle buzzer because we like the name beside it. Still nothing. Push the third, nothing; then the first again, with quick jabs as if sending a code. He thinks of jamming them with a stick or a nail he always seems to have in his pocket, picked up from the pile of nails the workmen on his house leave behind. Finally, we notice the tiniest of plaques off to one side, posting entrance hours. It's closed today? "Oh, no, this again," he groans. Just as we turn to leave, an angry shape materializes in the doorway of the cottage inside the gate. It's a heavy-set woman hanging out of the door like a conductor of a tram. She hollers something we can't understand. We back off and Soukup executes an exaggerated bow, which gets her shaking her head before she disappears, the door slamming behind her. When we bend around the wall's corner, Soukup suggests we consider jumping the wall in the vicinity of Kafka's grave, whose location he's not quite sure of, however. We also take note that the top of the wall is studded with jagged glass scraps. Our parting shot's a booming recitative; we sing the sign on a tree we can see inside: DR. FRANZ KAFKA! The black arrow at the bottom points to the right. The "Dr." sticks in our eyes, makes him seem even farther away. From the last time I was here, with a group of students in tow, I vaguely recall the grave is a hundred or so feet farther down the wall, so I figure we can at least get an approximate fix on the spot. I pull Soukup along till my arm shoots out like a divining rod. We put an ear to the wall. Nothing. Soukup whispers something in Czech, shakes his fist at the sky, and stiffly turns about, marching off with a look over his shoulder so I know to follow him. An old man, a stack of wreaths around his arm like hoops, comes right up to us. On an impulse we each buy one, dash back down the wall, and float them over, doffing our caps.

On the way back to the car we run into three huge Russian buses snorting to a stop. Out file what appear to be tourists. Two by two, arm in arm, they march down the sandy gravel through the cemetery's main gate. Before I understand what's what, Soukup loops his arm through mine and runs me along till we catch up to the Russians. Falling in behind as if the last couple in the entourage, we hurry along with them up and down rows of the immense site. Finally, the lead couple comes to a stop before a freshly turned grave and the rest of us fan out, fully three hundred of us waiting for a sign of what to do. Then we hear singing coming from three tiny figures approaching ever so slowly, swaying side to side, from the opposite gate at the far end of the lane. The closer they come the more we see they are priests of sorts. Circling the grave, they start chanting and the assembled hum along. Soukup and I look around for a casket, but none's in sight. Then someone starts sobbing and all three hundred join in, crying their hearts out. We can't help but add some wails, too. When we're all cried out, they follow the priests back to the buses, walking quickly and talking loudly among themselves. Soukup stops a gardener raking nearby and asks him what's going on, "exactly"—another word he likes to use a lot. I can see Soukup's having trouble getting through to the man, whose face in the slanting light now looks Mongoloid. "I know, I know," Soukup finally says to the man, and then whispers to me, "he's not able to help us, he's also clueless; but I wanted to keep talking with him for years," whereupon he asks me for the biggest coin I have and flips it to the man, who doffs his cap, stoops down for a large leaf, and hands it to Soukup. I know Soukup well enough by now: he'll have that leaf under glass on his mantel and expect daughter Denisa to cherish it long after he's gone.

"Okay, off we go now for some dog food or my hounds will get crazier than usual." After losing our way in a part of town the Soukups almost never visit, we wind up finding a building that looks like a blockhouse which needs a fresh coat of paint. The sign towering over the top says *"Maso"* (meat) in blue plastic letters.

When we exit the car, the smell clobbers us. Soukup dons some old gloves and removes a pail from the trunk. I hang behind till he comes back, flanked by a man and woman dressed, it seems, in nothing but caps and enormous, bloody aprons. The woman starts hosing down the cement. Soukup gives the man a bill and is handed the pail filled with brown bones and shreds of foul-smelling flesh. Just as we're about to drive off, a large Mercedes pulls up. The chauffeur repeats Soukup's routine, complete with gloves and pail.

"Karel, for Charlemagne's sake, isn't there a Purina Chow chain in town? You have to feed your pets like this?"

"Afraid so, Comrade. Mass-produced food for animals is a capitalist sin," he says sternly. "Of course, next time you come, please bring us as many boxes of dry dog food as possible, rather than cartons of cigarettes, not to mention those Tic Tacs you so kindly remembered. One of these days, I must have my addiction to them looked into." Now he's laughing and mock-crying.

We leave for last a discussion of his work, which my colleagues and I hope to collect in one edition for publication, perhaps even as a volume in a new translation series we've started at our college. We want readers to appreciate the range of this writer, not all that well known in English. When he comes to my room, he finds me surrounded by dictionaries, plump little things with the same soft red cover. He can't believe they were on the shelf above my cot: one for technical terms, another for idiomatic expressions, another on wildlife, still another on Old Czech. We both know we won't need them; it's a little play I'm staging to amuse him. "See, that's how we have to work on your pieces back home, Karel!" He sweeps the dictionaries aside, sits down on the cot, unwinding his scarf, and asks where to start in. On the texts I've already had help with back home, I suggest. I tell him the tale of how we found an honest-to-goodness Czech family, recently emigrated, who run Old Prague, a cozy restaurant in Vermilion, Ohio. My wife and I were eating there one night, and she suggested I find out from the folks in the kitchen—whom we could barely make out through the swinging doors—whether they or someone they know might be able to help with Soukup's particular brand of Czech. A rough understanding of possibilities in the original texts was what we were after. We'd had to give up on a scholar in Cleveland, who couldn't resist translating them academically, so that any sense of a human voice was lacking.

The woman was tending something like soup in a cauldron on an old-fashioned wood-burning stove in the steamy kitchen, bandana tight around her head, her face square, her arms burly as if made for stirring. She looked up. "What you want, please?" I stumbled through an explanation, and at the mention of Soukup's name, she stopped stirring, wiped her hands on her apron, and shook my hand hard. "Oh, is very great po-et, very great, we all know some poems he write. We be happy to help how we can, mister." So her whole family chipped in—even her husband, hanging out the screen door in an undershirt and a sailor's cap, looking like he could see straight across Lake Erie as far as Czechoslovakia; and also their teenagers, our waitresses, whose English was more fluent. They all worked on Soukup's texts that summer.

Soukup and I spent the next several hours going over all their efforts. He couldn't have been more interested in their solutions, even as he broke out in deep laughs when this or that word or expression had been totally misunderstood. "Not everyone in Prague, not to mention Pilsen where I grew up, knows what I mean. And of course I sometimes have no clue either. Didn't my favorite American poet, Levertov, say somewhere that unless there's a spot in your poem you don't quite understand, it's likely not a very good poem." Some moments are especially funny: a word I'd been told meant "monument to the dead" is just the name of a small burg near Prague! We discuss the process of misunderstanding and mistranslation. Soukup's genius, I can't help feeling, has something to do with his insisting we keep several mistranslations a Czech student made, and even one I contributed, because "the ideas are so beautiful I wish I'd thought of them!" He slaps his knee, fairly snorting a laugh that brings the landlady to the door.

What he takes great pains to clarify, above all, is the locus of the texts in Czech, especially who's talking to whom and why. Thus in one instance, if the English doesn't make clear it's a kindergarten teacher lecturing her pupils, the import's totally lost. So we turn phrases over and over, like a baker trying to get the lumps out. Sometimes, we put them back in! Finally, we're faced with what material to keep in the anthology and what to reject. My wife's little poem pops into mind, which I recite for Soukup: *Autumn – What shall go? / What shall stay?"* He loves the couplet, translating it immediately into Czech, making me learn it on the spot so I can say it back to her in Czech. By now we've gone way past a meal and are exhausted, at which point the landlady happens by again and knocks on my door to see if she can get us anything. Her husband on her heel, they begin tidying up around us nervously, almost as if we weren't there. When they leave, Soukup looks worried. They were too curious, sniffing around as they did, he thinks. But it's not till I start packing for my flight home that I realize things have been rearranged in my briefcase, and something I can't quite identify seems missing from a pocket in my suitcase. Papers I felt sure were in one section suddenly are in another. When Soukup picks me up for the drive to the airport I tell him everything: what seemed moved, as well as what seemed untouched. He's certain they're "piddling little agents" and lets go of the wheel a second, pretending to pray.

Soon we're out on the highway, airport-bound. Everything else starts to fade. I joke we might as well just keep driving, down to Senica, slip past the Russian tanks, to put a little stone on great

CZECHOSLOVAKIA

gramma's grave. Soukup laughs for another reason: do I know the one about Czech roads? It seems one surveying team started from Prague, the other from the border, and never the twain did meet! It might have been the cheap Russian equipment or the beer, who knows? "Anyway, prepare thyself," he pokes me in the ribs and jerks to a stop so my head almost hits the windshield. The road we'd been on stops on a dime, just stops! We have to trail off down a little dirt stretch, cross a rickety bridge before meeting up with the other ribbon of the pike that missed its mate by several hundred meters. "Oy to the Oyth," we sing in unison.

The airport's just waking up. We need a cup of coffee, but the bar's still closed so we spin around on the stools, exchanging last words. When I surprise him by asking if he'd ever consider replacing me for a year while I go on sabbatical, there's that signature laugh again; and it won't be for several years of thawing, then freezing, then thawing again that that actually comes to pass. Changing the subject, I wonder why so many people are standing in line at a shop at the end of the mall. "They're waiting for the morning paper," he says. "In fact, people actually drive out here for an early edition. Imagine, for the only official newspaper, sanctioned by the State, the one and only, the one they can't stop reading but no one trusts. But they'll stand in line in all weathers for hours, sometimes, hungry for any sign things might be changing. Of course," he adds in something of a whisper, "it helps if the president's wife dies in a helicopter crash, right here at the airport the night before."

Then the bar opens. We order coffee with a shot of cognac, and drink to the health of the president of the Democratic Republic of Czechoslovakia, the memory of his beloved wife, the grief of their whole family, the nation's grief, and may my plane not be more than the usual three or four hours delayed. It's time to check in, we hug hard and I shuffle down a long corridor. After clearing the security gate, I look back to see Soukup gripping its bars, his smile aglow, waving the little wave children do with half a hand.

July 14-15 / 1998

Still get confused trying to recall if my father died the day before Miroslav Holub or the day after. Could look it up, of course, but seem destined to dwell in the blur of their back-to-back deaths. No one's whispered "get over it" yet, or perhaps I would, as that's sometimes enough to redirect me.

We were at Dad's hospital in Milwaukee. He was having a hard time rehabbing from a broken hip. He'd called soon after falling down some steps to say he was jealous of my breaking mine some months before, and did I mind him writing a few verses about it? It was soon clear he was giving up, kept saying ninety-three years was way beyond the curve, anyway. Dr. Death, finished with the patient next door, had some pneumonia left over.

Rehabbing my hip, I'd watched older folks give up, beg the therapist to cut back on the ankle weights. I kept whispering in Dad's ear, "You can do it, I know you can. Just swing your good leg down and ..." He'd slowly turn his head side to side, other, older pains in his eyes. When we begged the attending to up Dad's morphine, he said he didn't want to be responsible for addicting him. "At ninety-three?" I yelled until a nurse came running.

To this day, I thank The One Above that our doctor daughter was along: she's never lacked the courage to argue with authority figures. Lo and behold, eventually more morphine dripped down Dad's line. She sent me to the lounge to nap when I fell asleep hand in hand with Dad, whose healing touch had once applied mustard plasters to my chest, steadied me in the shower to ease croup, and mortared and pestled compounds on the marble slab in his pharmacy for many a family's ills. His customers were as likely to seek his advice as the neighborhood doc's.

Coming across a few poems Dad had scrawled in an old prescription notebook, all I could think was Grandma Moses—because of their direct simplicity, their sure, no-nonsense strokes. I copied a few to send to Miroslav, who would salute the scientific detail, know the pharmacology was exact, even smile about their "deeply human sentiments"—words I never heard anyone utter as often as he did.

A week later, one of Miroslav's other translators called from London, and in a hoarse voice said, "Have you heard, our Holub is dead …"

His voice thickened. I could bite off just two words: "When? How?" He said Miroslav had been shaving one morning, getting ready to tour yet another country, when Jitka, his wife, heard the razor strike the floor. Moments later she found him dead. An embolism, apparently. Oddly, I couldn't help thinking how Miroslav would have described the dynamics of incurring a fatal embolism.

Soon I was awash in memories of our many brotherly encounters, going back some twenty years to the first, in Prague. I'd gone for help translating his poems which, like the omentum he and his research team studied, bore the indelible traces of life's assault on body and soul.

Many scientists and writers predicted he'd win Nobels in literature and biology in the same year; but of all his numerous honors and prizes, I know he especially cherished the Honorary Degree Oberlin College bestowed. He'd taught here several times, once even chairing The Writing Program when I was on leave. He found the experience "tremendous"—another of his favorite English words, which he'd almost sing out. To this day, his former students cherish their memories of working with him;

JULY 14-15 / 1998

and his work enjoys a tremendous following among them.

As Andrei Voznesensky was a guest of Oberlin's president at the time, someone got the problematic idea to give honorary degrees to him and Miroslav at the same time, as well as ask them to write poems for the commencement ceremony. Many did not know that, as president of the Soviet Writer's Union, Voznesensky could and on at least one occasion might have caused a book of Miroslav's poems to be stopped mid-publication. Miroslav's anxiety was palpable, and I was not looking forward to driving them together to the staging area, where they'd have to line up side by side for the march past the graduating class on to the dais.

"Comrade," I could hear Voznesensky say to Miroslav in the back seat, "my ulcer is acting up. You are a medical doctor, can you prescribe something?"

"Esteemed Comrade," Miroslav said ever so softly, his words still in my ear, "nothing will help if you do not cut back on your drinking." Miroslav's mouth—I could see in the rearview mirror—was slightly ajar, his tongue brushing his lips. Without another word between them, Voznesensky turned to stare out his window, while Miroslav stared out his.

The headline in the papers the next day could have read: "Dueling Poems." It was abundantly clear from the competing texts they were trying to outdo each other. If you look up their poems in the college archives—the Russian and Czech originals, alongside their translations—you will clearly see each poet's way with the genetics of his poetics: one with the precise observation and incisive wit of a great scientist; the other brimming with the hortatory of the Russian temperament.

My paternal grandmother was Czech by birth, so from time to time I'd send my father translations of Miroslav's poems Dana Habová and I were collaborating on. Dad also treasured a picture volume of the landscape around her birthplace in Senica, which

Miroslav once took my cousin and me to visit, and where he'd uncovered some of our family's genealogy. Here's the Holub poem that moved my father the most:

AUTUMN

And it's all over.

No more sweetpeas,
no more wide-eyed bunnies
dropping from the sky.

Only
a reddish boniness
under the sun of hoarfrost,
a thievish fog,
an insipid solution of love
            hate
                and crowing.

But next year
The larches will try
to make the land full of larches again
and larks will try
to make the land full of larks.

And thrushes will try
to make all the trees sing,
and goldfinches will try
to make all the grass golden,

JULY 14-15 / 1998

*and burying beetles
with their creaky love will try
to make all the corpses
rise from the dead.*

Amen.

CPSIA information can be obtained
at www.ICGtesting.com
Printed in the USA
FFOW03n2114140417
34483FF